A CHRISTMAS
GARLAND

A CHRISTMAS
GARLAND *woven*

by MAX BEERBOHM

with illustrations by the author
and an introduction by

N. JOHN HALL

1993

NEW HAVEN AND LONDON

YALE UNIVERSITY PRESS

Grateful acknowledgment is made to Mrs Eva Reichmann for permission to publish this work. Plates are published by kind permission of the following: Ashmolean Museum, Oxford, Nos. 2, 6, 10, 17, 20, 21, 24; Charterhouse School, No. 7; Cornell University Library, No. 19; Houghton Library, Harvard University, Nos. 4, 22; Mr Mark Samuels Lasner, Nos. 9, 15; Merton College Library, Oxford, Nos. 11, 12; Harry Ransom Humanities Research Center, University of Texas at Austin, No. 13; Mr James B. Sitrick, No. 8; Robert H. Taylor Collection, Princeton University Library, Nos. 1, 3, 5, 14, 16, 18, 23, and all eight in-text title-pages.

CARICATURES

"IMPROVED" TITLE-PAGES

INTRODUCTION

Parody is often thought of as an art under a cloud, derivative and unfriendly. And parody in an obvious way does depend on a particular source, and its ridicule of that source is in some sense hostile. But in the hands of a Max Beerbohm parody can become, in Dwight Macdonald's words, "an intuitive kind of literary criticism, shorthand for what 'serious' critics must write out at length." It can be even more than this; it can be a species of imaginative writing, a kind of comic art that enjoys a life of its own.

Literary parody goes back at least as far as Aristophanes, but few writers have ever possessed in quite equal degree what Max Beerbohm wryly dubbed his "rather dreadful little talent" for this art, and there has never been a better collection of parodies in English than *A Christmas Garland* (so named because a Christmas theme, however slight or oblique, unites the seventeen sketches). Why then is the book not more widely appreciated? One reason is that prejudice against parody, a prejudice which partakes of the general bias favoring the "serious" over the humorous, the tragic over the comic—an error so old that it hardly seems worthwhile contradicting. Another reason arises from the fact that some of the writers parodied in *A Christmas Garland* are not well known, and in order to appreciate parody the reader is supposed to have some familiarity with the author being parodied. While many people today are conversant with James, Shaw, Hardy, and

INTRODUCTION

Conrad, fewer than one would expect actually read much of Kipling, Meredith, Wells, Bennett, or Galsworthy; and most people today know nothing at all of A. C. Benson, G. S. Street, or Maurice Hewlett. Still, not knowing the target of the parody isn't as large a drawback as one might expect. As Lawrence Danson has argued, Max's parodies of George Moore and Frank Harris, for example, "extort ironic self-revelations" from these writers, and the "resulting spectacle remains comic despite the obscurity of its subject." In their self-absorption, their self-ignorance, we recognize the human type. Hence the parodies of complete unknowns can be enjoyable in their own right: reading G. S. Str**t's essay, one sees immediately, and with amusement, that Street was a meanderer, a writer who went down little by-ways, losing his way for the time being but not caring, coming back to his point (if any) later, and no apologies offered. Naturally, most readers will find the parodies of their own favorite writers more delicious, and for some the imitations of a handful of those favorites—of James, Conrad, and Kipling, for instance—are enough to make the book a treasure. Moreover, *A Christmas Garland* is so rich a work that, rather like the Scriptures, it is best looked into for brief spells. One should not try to read all seventeen parodies through in one gulp.

An editor's preface to a book such as this, while not trying to explain jokes, can be helpful by providing some background and a taste of what is being parodied. The authors imitated here flourished while Max himself flourished, in the 1890s and the early years of the twentieth century. The book was published in 1912, at the height of his career, two years after he married and "retired" to Rapallo, Italy. All of the writers parodied

INTRODUCTION

were known to him personally, and many were good friends. With a few notable exceptions, he admired them and their works. He maintained that he parodied and caricatured subjects that he loved. This was not entirely true, as we shall see. In any case, we do know some of the particulars of what Max thought of his subjects, both as men and as writers, and in a few instances we know what they thought of the parodies. Such knowledge is not indispensable for the reading of this book, but it is welcome.

HENRY JAMES

Pride of place went to Henry James (1843–1916), Max's favorite novelist, and this in spite of the fact that he sometimes complained, like everyone else, of the difficulties of James's later, more convoluted style. The parody of that late style, "The Mote in the Middle Distance," an account of two children, Keith and Eva Tantalus, debating whether to "peer" into their Christmas stockings, has attained a kind of classic status, and may be the most anthologized parody in the language. Any passage taken at random is redolent of the Master. Listen to the opening lines:*

It was with the sense of a, for him, very memorable something that he peered now into the immediate

---

* Equally convincing is the partial sentence that forms the caption for the caricature (Plate 1) of Henry James in a thick London fog looking closely at his hand: "...It was, therefore, not without something of a shock that he, in this to him so very congenial atmosphere, now perceived that a vision of the hand which he had, at a venture, held up within an inch or so of his eyes was, with an almost awful clarity being adumbrated..."

INTRODUCTION

future, and tried, not without compunction, to take that period up where he had, prospectively, left it. But just where the deuce *had* he left it? The consciousness of dubiety was, for our friend, not, this morning, quite yet clean-cut enough to outline the figures on what she had called his "horizon," between which and himself the twilight was indeed of a quality somewhat intimidating.

John Felstiner, who sees Keith and Eva largely as a burlesque of Merton Densher and Kate Croy in the final scene of *The Wings of the Dove*, writes perceptively:

> All the turns of style Beerbohm invents for Keith and Eva can be found in *The Wings of the Dove* and *The Golden Bowl*. They sometimes seem to be done better by Beerbohm, sometimes less well done: the broken sentences, roundabout simplicities, syntactical quibbles, colloquialisms made genteel by inverted commas, italics for delicate intonation, stunning double negatives, accumulated homely adjectives, abruptly placed, vague adverbs, banal metaphors worried and reworried, the narrator's unsettling glances into the future and his intimacy with "our friend" Keith, the exasperating, magnified scruples, and, at last, the vibrant moral renunciation by Keith and Eva—"One doesn't violate the shrine—pick the pearl from the shell!"

Max feared that James, a friend but not an intimate, might have resented the parody, but James read it with "wonder and delight," calling the book "the most intelligent that has been produced in England for many a long day." James, who asked Edmund Gosse to convey these

INTRODUCTION

sentiments to Max, went on to say that the parodies were
so good that none of the writers satirized in *A Christmas
Garland* could now write "without incurring the reproach of somewhat ineffectively imitating" Max. He
expressed the same views to Sydney Waterlow, calling
the book "a little masterpiece," declaring himself de-
lighted with the parody of himself, and saying that now
whenever he wrote he felt he was "parodying himself."
The notion that the parodied writers would henceforth
run the risk of being charged with "somewhat inef-
fectually imitating" Max raises a curious issue. It has
become a byword of criticism that "Max," the writer
created by Max Beerbohm, is somehow discernibly present in every line he wrote, especially in his essays. But if
in *A Christmas Garland* he so wondrously enters not
only into the styles and mannerisms but into the very
minds, so to speak, of his subjects, is he himself still
there? The reader seems to hear in these imitations both
the parodied writer and the parodist; one recognizes
Henry James's late prose, sounding more like James than
James himself often does, but one also catches the voice
of the antic "Max" throughout the whole performance.
It's difficult to say how this is so unless one returns to
the notion of parody as criticism. Some remarks of
Filson Young in "The Perfect Parodist," a review of the
book on its first appearance in 1912, touch upon this
question. Young, after saying that Max has "not so much
copied his models as extended them," insists that Max's
"delicate exaggerations" reveal not only weakness but
"forces" in his victims' writings:

> It is as though, instead of elaborately describing the
> clothes worn by his subjects, Max had himself put on

each suit in turn, strutted or lounged awhile in the manner of each, and spoken thoughts like theirs in a telling imitation of their tones. And behind these solemn parodies of Kipling, Henry James, Wells, Meredith and so forth lurks the shadow of Max himself, making it quite plain to you in what estimation each is held and mocking with a merciful humour the mannerisms of them all.

This, it seems to me, is just right. Behind the parodies of James and Meredith, however funny, however cruel, one discovers admiration, even reverence; behind the parody of Wells, one detects disagreement, distaste; behind the parody of Benson, one senses bemusement (as Max said in another connection, "One should be grateful to any man who makes himself ridiculous"); behind the parody of Kipling, one feels genuine dislike, hostility.

RUDYARD KIPLING

The second parody is of the writer Max least admired among his seventeen subjects. Rudyard Kipling (1865–1936) was Beerbohm's *bête noire.* "To me," he wrote, "who gets the finest of all literary joy out of Henry James . . . the sort of person that Kipling is, and the sort of thing that Kipling does, cannot strongly appeal—quite the contrary. I carefully guard myself by granting you that Kipling is a genius. . . . The *schoolboy*, the *bounder*, and the *brute*—these three types have surely never found a more brilliant expression of themselves than in R. K. . . . But as a poet and seer R. K. seems to me not to exist, except for the purpose of contempt." Max detested "the smell of blood, beer, and 'baccy'" that he found exuding from Kipling's pages. Kipling he saw as "the Apocalyptic Bounder who can do such fine things but mostly prefers to stand (on tip-toe and stridently) for all that is cheap and nasty."* Max especially disliked Kipling's "manliness." Reviewing a theater production of an early Kipling novel, *The Light that Failed*, adapted for the stage by Julia Constance Fletcher, writing under the name "George Fleming," he wickedly suggested that "Rudyard Kipling" might also be a pseudonym for a woman. In *The Light that Failed*, Max says,

> men are portrayed ... from an essentially feminine point of view. They are men seen from the outside, or rather, not seen at all, but feverishly imagined.... "*My* men—*my* men!" cries Dick Heldar when a regiment of soldiers passes his window. He is not their commanding officer. He was at one time a war-correspondent.... He had always doted on the military. And so has Mr. Kipling. To him, as to his hero, they typify, in its brightest colours, the notion of manhood, manliness, man. And by this notion Mr. Kipling is permanently and joyously obsessed. That is why I say that his standpoint is feminine.

In novels written by men, Max contends, "virility is taken for granted"; in novels by (inept) woman writers, the male characters are constantly acting in a "manly" fashion, ever in dread "of a sudden soprano note in the

---

* Compare Oscar Wilde's more favorable verdict on (early) Kipling: reading him is like "reading life by superb flashes of vulgarity.... From the point of view of literature Mr. Kipling is a genius who drops his aspirates. From the point of view of life, he is a reporter who knows vulgarity better than any one has ever known it.... He is our first authority on the second-rate." ("The Critic as Artist")

bass"; "They must, at all costs, be laconic, taciturn, as becomes men. Their language must be strong but sparse.... In real life, men are not like that. At least, only the effeminate men are like that. The others have no preoccupation with manliness. They don't bother about it." And so Max finds it remarkable that "these heroes, with their self-conscious blurtings of oaths and slang, their cheap cynicism about the female sex, their mutual admiration for one another's display of all those qualities ... were not ... fondly created out of the inner consciousness of a lady-novelist." Miss Fletcher offers "a marvelously close adaptation of the book," Max says, capturing the "inconfusible" vulgarity that is Kiplingese (though he regrets that she omitted "Dick's immortal description of his inamorata as 'a bilious little thing'").

A few passages from the novel show precisely the side of Kipling that Beerbohm so loathed. *The Light that Failed*, the story of a war artist who loses his sight, is filled to overflowing with bloodshed, the glory of war, and the delights of what today is called "male bonding." Here is part of the description of the skirmish in the Sudan in which the hero, Dick Heldar, receives the blow that eventually blinds him:

> Dick was conscious that somebody had cut him violently across his helmet, that he had fired his revolver into a black, foam-flecked face which forthwith ceased to bear any resemblance to a face, and that Torpenhow [his fellow war correspondent] had gone down under an Arab whom he had tried to "collar low," and was turning over and over with his captive, feeling for the man's eyes.... [Torpenhow] had shaken himself clear of his enemy, and rose,

wiping his thumb on his trousers. The Arab, both hands to his forehead, screamed aloud, then snatched up his spear and rushed at Torpenhow, who was panting under the shelter of Dick's revolver. Dick fired twice, and the man dropped limply. His upturned face lacked one eye. The musketry-fire redoubled, but cheers mingled with it. The rush had failed, and the enemy were flying.

When Dick and Torpenhow are reunited in London, "Dick burst into his room, to be received with a hug which nearly cracked his ribs." Towards the end of the story, Dick, now completely sightless from the wound received earlier, finds his way back to renewed fighting in the Sudan. As British soldiers are firing on the natives from a train, Dick hears the "unlimited howling" of the stricken Arabs outside, and stretches himself on the floor, wild with delight at the sounds and the smells. " 'God is very good—I never thought I'd hear this again. Give 'em hell, men. Oh, give 'em hell!' he cried." At the novel's close, one reads that "[Dick's] luck had held to the last, even to the crowning mercy of a kindly bullet through his head."

The Light that Failed is so extreme in its blood and gore, patriotism, imperialism, and "manliness" that one reading it today thinks for just a moment that it may be satiric or farcical; but it's deadly serious. Max attacks this side of Kipling in his parody, "P.C., X, 36," a light spoof, complete with a "Police Station Ditty," a perfect imitation in dialect of Kipling's own "Departmental Ditties" and "Barrack Room Ballads." In the parody, a brutal and jingoistic policeman, Judlip, having lamented that Christmas Eve "ain't wot it was," he having not had

as much as a lost dog to kick, perks up when he arrests
and manhandles Santa Claus, whom he has caught
emerging from a chimney—the Kipling-like narrator
urging him on and accusing the victim of being a German.
For all its fun, a palpable hostility characterizes the
sketch. Here, certainly, one finds little of the "reverence"
or the "mocking what one loves" that Max himself
claimed as his inspiration for caricature and parody.

A. C. BENSON

Arthur Christopher Benson (1862–1925), Master of
Magdalene College, Cambridge, and man of letters, is
today among the least remembered of Max's subjects
(his brother E. F. Benson has held up better). A. C.
Benson wrote more than a hundred volumes—
biographies, literary criticism, poetry, fiction, essays.
Among these his essays were most popular, although
a sympathetic *DNB* entry on Benson called them "somewhat tenuous in substance" and predicted they were
"unlikely to last." Max's parody—Benson was said
to have been a little hurt by it—follows Benson's loose
discursive style as exemplified in *From a College
Window* (1906). The essays are vague, meandering, sentimental, self-indulgent; an apt word for their contents
would surely be *harmless*, something Max captures
neatly in his title, "Out of Harm's Way." In his essays
Benson seems a kind of apostle of the obvious; moreover,
if at any time he makes a statement of the slightest force,
he immediately qualifies it. (The parody includes the
sentence "He never condemned a thing.") Since readers
today are utterly unfamiliar with the originals, a couple

INTRODUCTION

of paragraphs typical of Benson are given here, from an essay entitled "On Growing Older":

> I have a theory that one ought to grow older in a tranquil and appropriate way, that one ought to be perfectly contented with one's time of life, that amusements and pursuits ought to alter naturally and easily, and not be regretfully abandoned. One ought not to be dragged protesting from the scene, catching desperately at every doorway and balustrade; one should walk off smiling. It is easier said than done. It is not a pleasant moment when a man first recognises that he is out of place on the football field, that he cannot stoop with the old agility to pick up a skimming stroke to cover-point, that dancing is rather too heating to be decorous, that he cannot walk all day without undue somnolence after dinner, or rush off after a heavy meal without indigestion. These are sad moments which we all of us reach, but which are better laughed over than fretted over.

After many such pages the essay draws to a close:

> And thus I went slowly back to College in the gathering gloom that seldom fails to bring a certain peace of mind. . . . So when I entered my booklined rooms, and heard the kettle sing its comfortable song on the hearth, and reflected that I had a few letters to write, an interesting book to turn over, a pleasant Hall dinner to look forward to, and that, after a space of talk, an undergraduate or two coming to talk over a leisurely piece of work, an essay or a paper, I was more than ever inclined to acquiesce in my disabilities, to purr like an elderly cat, and to feel that

while I had the priceless boon of leisure, set in a framework of small duties, there was much to be said for life, and that I was a poor creature if I could not be soberly content.

The reviewer for the *Spectator* in 1912 judged the Benson parody the best piece in *A Christmas Garland*. Another reviewer, in a notice of the 1950 edition, aptly described Max's mimicry of Benson's "chronic dribble of harmless unnecessary musings" as "lethal."*

Max drew caricatures of all the writers parodied in *A Christmas Garland* (of George Moore, a favorite subject, he drew some thirty caricatures). The one caricature he is known to have made of Benson has unfortunately disappeared. From its caption the drawing sounds as though it must have been a treat, and a good companion piece to the parody: "Mr Arthur Christopher Benson vowing eternal fidelity to the obvious."

H. G. WELLS

Max was on good terms with H. G. Wells (1866–1946), but had no sympathy with his faith in science or his social idealism. S. N. Behrman wrote of Max that he "shied away from lunacy not only in its violent forms but

---

* Privately, Max also made fun in verse of Benson's essays:

> No dips in my ample tub of bran
>   Bring aught but bran to light:
> You'ld think I *must* be a clergyman,
>   So like one do I write.
>
> From "Triolets by A.C.B."

INTRODUCTION

also in its milder forms, one of these being utopianism.
'Good sense about trivialities is better than nonsense
about things that matter,' he once said. He had a horror
of utopians, a suspicion of 'big' ideas." Wells's prose
troubled him as well. Writing to Shaw in 1903, Max took
the view that "the literary gift is a mere accident—is as
often bestowed on idiots who have nothing to say worth
hearing as it is denied to strenuous sages.... How about
H. G. Wells, for example? *There*'s an evangelist and a
seer, indisputably. But his writing! Have you ever seen a
cold rice-pudding spilt on the pavement of Gower Street?
I never have. But it occurs to me as a perfect simile for
Wells's writing." In 1921, when Reggie Turner sent Max a
copy of Wells's *History of the World,* he replied, "You
couldn't have given me a present that I should have
hated more."

The parody, "Perkins and Mankind" (a very Wellsian
title), published originally in 1906, is actually two
parodies. The young protagonist Perkins, a reforming
MP, visits the country house of a duke and duchess,
where the guests include many lords and ladies, plus the
"usual lot from the Front Benches and the Embassies,"
and others clearly "above" him socially. This Christmas
party marks a "turning-point" in his career. Already
saddened by the failure of his Bill for the "Provisional
Government of England by the Female Foundlings,"
he is further disillusioned as he observes the useless
existence of the aristocratic and ruling classes: "They
were up to nothing whatever." He refuses to wear the
diamond and sapphire sleeve-links that are his Christmas
present from the duchess. "No, damn it!" he says under
his breath, vowing not to let these people "use" him. He
has just about given up trying to right the "huge nasty

INTRODUCTION

mess" the human race has made of things, when later, in
his room, he finds a copy of "Sitting Up For The Dawn,"
one of a series of sociological tracts by H. G. W*lls. Here
was the work that "had first touched his soul to finer
issues." He reads from the book—the quoted passages
are about as long as the story itself—and it "re-exert[s]
its old sway over him." He determines to keep trying to
reform the world, and he leaves a note to his hostess
excusing himself on the grounds of "urgent political
business."

Perkins reminds one somewhat of Kipps from Wells's
delightful comic novel of that name, published a year
before the parody. But whereas Perkins is obviously
educated and accomplished (at least he's in Parlia-
ment), Kipps is not only irredeemably "lower-class" in
his speech and habits, but also slow-witted, plodding,
clumsy, unprepossessing. On the other hand, Kipps, suddenly rich from an unexpected legacy, resembles Perkins
in discovering himself lured to the society of his social
betters, where he becomes disenchanted and opts out.
He does so first at an "Anagram Tea":

> [Kipps] found himself being introduced to people, and
> then he was in a corner with the short lady in a big
> bonnet, who was pelting him with gritty little bits of
> small talk that were gone before you could take hold
> of them and reply.... What a chatter they were all
> making! It was just like a summer sale [at the haber-
> dasher's where he had been apprenticed].... And
> suddenly the smouldering fires of rebellion leapt to
> flame again. These were a rotten lot of people, and the
> anagrams were rotten nonsense, and he, Kipps, had
> been a rotten fool to come....

INTRODUCTION

He was going to get out of it all!... "I'm orf," he said.
"Desh it!" he cries, throwing away his anagram placard.
Shortly afterwards he attends a lofty dinner party, and
mid-way through:

> For once in his life he had distinctly made up his mind
> on his own account.... He put down his knife and
> fork and refused anything that followed.... He had,
> in fact, burnt his boats and refused to join the
> ladies.... "I got something to do," he said.

Kipps retreats to his old life and his old girl, a servant.

"Sitting Up For The Dawn," the parody within the
parody, draws on various social writings by Wells, but
most specifically on *A Modern Utopia*, published, like
Kipps, in 1905. (It is difficult now to realize the influence
Wells exerted at this time. Reviewers called *A Modern
Utopia* a "masterpiece," claimed it was "the most interesting, imaginative, and possible of all utopias written
since the inventions and discoveries of science began to
colour our conceptions of the future"; one notice went
so far as to place it at "the head of the long list of works
of its class, beginning with Plato's 'Republic'.") Wells's
Utopia, a parallel world to our own but on a distant
planet, is a World State: it allows no private property in
land or natural objects; it has universal education, a
world language, world-wide travel, world-wide "freedom
of sale and purchase," and "universally diffused good
manners"; it boasts mechanical advances such as elec-
trical heating of floors, walls, and beds, self-cleaning
rooms, and two-hundred-mile-per-hour monorails. Fac-
tory labor is pleasant, with "cessation" of work at noon;
the workers experience none of that "brooding stress

that pursues the worker on earth, that caring anxiety that drives him so often to stupid betting, stupid drinking, and violent and mean offenses." Everyone seems in good health: "one rarely meets fat people, bald people, or bent or grey." Max's parody takes *A Modern Utopia* a step further: "General Cessation Day," the chapter Perkins happens upon in "Sitting Up For The Dawn," explains the nearest equivalent of Christmas in the Utopian future. It's the one day in the thousand-day year—the week has ten days, the month fifty days, a system not much more peculiar than Wells's "duodecimal system of counting"— when the entire population has a holiday from work (throughout the year everyone rests on one day in ten, but each tenth of the population has a different "Cessation" day). This "General Cessation Day" is marked by the ceremony of "Making Way" in which old people march cheerfully off to the Municipal Lethal Chamber. It's not too unimaginable in the world of *A Modern Utopia*, with its many rules and restrictions on parenthood, its isolation of criminals, its unfairness to women, its rule by the elite *summarai*, the governing and professional class (and sole voters), who are re- stricted to a prescribed regimen of healthful food, and are forbidden tobacco and alcohol, along with such flamboyant activities as "acting, singing, or reciting." "Sitting Up For The Dawn," complete with its Wells-style footnotes—a good number of them to his own works— takes on the style of Wells's scientific and social writing. Derek Stanford finds here "all the coarse over-confident side" of Wells's social writing and in the Perkins story the "element of insensitiveness—of a vulgar unaware- ness of vulgarity," with both parodies pointing up "Wells's weakness of taste, of discretion." One small,

typical particular: Wells makes constant use of the
homely phrase "You figure . . ." (in the sense of "picture"
or "see in your mind"), and sure enough, in "Sitting Up
For The Dawn," one comes upon it four times in five
pages.

G. K. CHESTERTON

Max was fond of G. K. Chesterton (1874–1936) and, with
reservations, he admired his books, at least the early
ones. But Chesterton's ambitious religious and social
views, many of which he shared with his friend Hilaire
Belloc, were not to his liking. In old age Max said of the
two: "They had blind spots, but they were delightful men.
Such enormous gusto, you know, such gaiety, and feeling
for life." Chesterton, who started life as a journalist (and
always gloried in the title), eventually published more
than a hundred books: fiction, poetry, religious and political works. When he appeared with much brilliance on
the London literary scene, Max, in 1902, went out of
his way to meet him and noted down his impressions:
"Enormous apparition. Head big for body—way of sink-
ing head on chest. Like a mountain and a volcanic one—
constant streams of talk flowing down—paradoxes flung
up into the air—very magnificent." Max's parody, "Some
Damnable Errors about Christmas," first published in
1906, probably took most of its inspiration from *Heretics*
(1905)—although it can be seen as drawing on innumer-
able other essays; in fact, such was Max's talent for
"divining," and such were Chesterton's consistencies,
that the parody seems also to draw on material as yet
unwritten. *Heretics* contains an essay titled "Christmas
and the Aesthetes" which, although not the single orig-

inal for "Some Damnable Errors about Christmas"—it being Max's practice to read extensively in his authors and then write in their fashion—can serve well to demonstrate Chesterton's style, his methods and mannerisms, along with a handful of his leading themes. One such theme was Christianity: Chesterton, at this time Anglo-Catholic (he was to become a Roman Catholic in 1922, after years of encouragement from Belloc— see Plate 18), was a life-long Christian apologist; but Chesterton's Christianity, like his liberalism, always had a youthful, rollicking, jolly, optimistic, almost prankish note to it. The same essay also exhibits his delight in opposites: good/evil, right/wrong, optimism/pessimism, old/new, rational/irrational, folly/wisdom, material/spiritual—always seen from some paradoxical angle, often with surprising insight, together with homely, incongruous examples offered to bolster his thesis. The argument of "Christmas and the Aesthetes" is that new or "undenominational" religions borrow from old religions but usually borrow the wrong things. Chesterton's examples are the Salvation Army and the philosophy of Auguste Comte:

> The usual verdict of educated people on the Salvation Army is expressed in some such words as these: "I have no doubt they do a great deal of good, but they do it in a vulgar and profane style; their aims are excellent, but their methods are wrong." To me, unfortunately, the precise reverse of this appears to be the truth. I do not know whether the aims of the Salvation Army are excellent, but I am quite sure their methods are admirable.... No one, perhaps, but a sociologist can see whether General Booth's housing

scheme is right. But any healthy person can see that banging brass cymbals together must be right.... And so while the philanthropy of the Salvationists and its genuineness may be a reasonable matter for the discussion of the doctors, there can be no doubt about the genuineness of their brass bands, for a brass band is purely spiritual....

And the same antithesis exists about another modern religion—I mean the religion of Comte, generally known as Positivism, or the worship of humanity. Such men as Mr Frederick Harrison, that brilliant and chivalrous philosopher [Chesterton always says something nice about his opponents]... would tell us that he offers us the philosophy of Comte, but not all Comte's fantastic proposals for pontiffs and ceremonials, the new calendar, the new holidays and saints' days. He does not mean that we should dress ourselves up as priests of humanity or let off fireworks because it is Milton's birthday. To the solid English Comtist all this appears, he confesses, to be a little absurd. To me it appears the only sensible part of Comtism.... If Comtism had spread the world would have been converted, not by the Comtist philosophy, but by the Comtist calendar.... I myself, to take a *corpus vile*, am very certain that I would not read the works of Comte through for any consideration whatever. But I can easily imagine myself with the greatest enthusiasm lighting a bonfire on Darwin Day.

Rationalists haven't succeeded because they lack festivals; they have no Christmas: "Mr. Swinburne does not hang up his stocking on the eve of the birthday of Victor

Hugo. Mr. William Archer does not sing carols descriptive of the infancy of Ibsen outside people's doors in the snow."

In Max's parody, replete with opposites—human/divine, present/past, love/hate—Ch*st*rt*n argues that since people have loved Christmas, they are most wrong about it: "If mankind had hated Christmas, he would have understood it from the first"; and because G. B. Shaw and his school, "with all their splendid sincerity and acumen," have failed to grasp this "basic principle that lies at the root of all things human and divine," they miss "all the mystery of the jolly visible world, and of that still jollier world which is invisible." Two examples are offered of "the more obvious fallacies" concerning Christmas:

> One is that Christmas should be observed as a time of jubilation.... It never entered into the heads of the Three Wise Men. They did not bring their gifts as a joke, but as an awful oblation.... I find myself in agreement with the cynics in so far that I admit that Christmas, as now observed, tends to create melancholy. But the reason for this lies solely in our own misconception. Christmas is essentially a *dies irae*. If the cynics will only make up their minds to treat it as such, even the saddest and most atrabilious of them will acknowledge that he has had a rollicking day.

(The occasional big word was also part of Chesterton's style: *atrabilious* here, *corybantic* in the "Aesthetes" essay). The other damnable error is the belief that "Christmas comes but once a year."

INTRODUCTION

THOMAS HARDY

Thomas Hardy (1840–1928), after achieving fame as a novelist, and after being allegedly disaffected from novel-writing by critical reviews of *Jude the Obscure*, returned to the ambition of his youth, poetry. Between 1903 and 1908 he brought out, in three volumes, a drama, mostly in iambic pentameter, the title page of which is self-describing: *The Dynasts: An Epic-Drama of the War with Napoleon, in Three Parts, Nineteen Acts, & One Hundred & Thirty Scenes, The Time Covered by the Action Being About Ten Years*. It was intended, as Hardy said, "simply for mental performance, and not for the stage."

The Dynasts has a cast of what seems to be thousands of characters, with the addition, as Hardy explains in his preface, of various "Spirits" or "supernatural spectators," certain "impersonated abstractions, or Intelligences," who comment on the action: they include the Spirit of the Years, the Spirit of the Pities, Spirits Sinister and Ironic, the Spirit of Rumour, all with attendant choruses, plus spirit messengers and recording angels. By this system Hardy wanted to give "the modern expression of a modern outlook." That is to say, Hardy is on his hobby horse, the question of purpose in the universe, those huge mysteries of Luck, Chance, Will, and Fate that he addressed so pessimistically throughout his career. *The Dynasts* opens in the "Overworld" of these spirits where the Shade of the Earth asks about the "Immanent Will and Its designs" and is answered by the Spirit of the Years:

> *It works unconsciously, as heretofore,*
> *Eternal artistries in Circumstance,*

INTRODUCTION

Whose patterns, wrought by rapt aesthetic rote,
Seem in themselves Its single listless aim,
And not their consequence.

And so on, for 500 closely-printed pages. The historical human characters speak intelligibly, but the Spirits often engage in affected, antiquated, sometimes arcane talk.

In 1904 Max wrote a review of *The Dynasts: Part First* that see-saws between praise and protest. He first comments on the hugeness of Hardy's subject: "To do perfectly what he essays would need a syndicate of much greater poets than ever were born into the world, working in an age of miracles." Given the unwieldy scope of the work, it is not surprising that the humans appear puny and negligible. They are "automata," whom Hardy wishes to show "not merely as they appear to certain supernal, elemental spirits, but also blindly obedient to an Immanent Will." After reading the book, Max says, we at first wonder why Hardy wrote it (or rather, we regret "that the Immanent Will put him to the trouble of writing it"). But that mood passes and we come to realize that we have been reading "a really great book"—an imperfect book, because although Hardy is undeniably a poet, "his poetry expresses itself much more surely and finely through the medium of prose." *The Dynasts*, Max goes on, is the first modern work of dramatic fiction to deny free-will to its characters. Nevertheless, Hardy's puppets are exciting:

> Free-will is not necessary to human interest. Belief in it is, however, necessary to human life. Cries Mr Hardy's Spirit of the Pities

INTRODUCTION

'This tale of Will
And Life's impulsion by Incognizance
I cannot take.'

Nor can I. But I take and treasure, with all gratitude, the book in which that tale is told so finely.

Max's "Sequelula to 'The Dynasts'" limits itself to the Spirits, who, spotting Earth's solar system in the Void, come to recall that they once visited the planet and observed its parasites, especially one called Napoleon. They become curious to learn what "another parasite" has recently written about their supposedly private visit. The Recording Angel orders up a copy of *The Dynasts* from the Superstellar Library and reads the book aloud to the Spirits. At first, under the influence of Mr Clement Shorter "and Chorus of Subtershorters" (Clement Shorter, journalist, editor, and Hardy enthusiast, had an obsession with Napoleon), they approve:

SPIRIT OF THE PITIES.

It is a book which, once you take it up,
You cannot readily lay down.

SPIRIT SINISTER.

There is
Not a dull page in it.

SPIRIT OF THE YEARS.

A bold conception
Outcarried with that artistry for which
The author's name is guarantee.

But, detecting and expelling Shorter, they are angered at Hardy's presumptuousness and deny any correlation

INTRODUCTION

between themselves and Hardy's depictions of them—
that is, they, like the critics, find him too depressingly
pessimistic. The Spirit of the Years complains:

> *I never said they were "automata"*
> *And "jackaclocks," nor dared describe their deeds*
> *As "Life's Impulsion by Incognizance."*
> *It may be that those mites have no free will,*
> *But how should I know?*

The Spirit of the Pities says:

> *The author of "The Dynasts" has indeed*
> *Misused his undeniably great gifts*
> *In striving to belittle things that are*
> *Little enough already.*

The Spirits decide to revisit the Earth to observe the
human race again, but this time at Christmas, which they
understand is a once-a-year festival in which "every
biped is beaming/With peace and good will" ("and why
not with free will?" the Semichorus asks). But the Spirit
of Mr Hardy guides them to a prison on the outskirts of
Casterbridge where they observe a scene of regimented
convicts being marched mechanically into chapel. Hor-
rified, the Spirits rush away, taking back their earlier
criticism of Hardy:

> *He was right.*
> *Automata these animalculae*
> *Are—puppets, pitiable jackaclocks.*
> *Be't as it may elsewhere, upon this planet*
> *There's no free will, only obedience*
> *To some blind, deaf, unthinking despotry*
> *That justifies the horridest pessimism.*

INTRODUCTION

In a signed footnote at the beginning of the "Se-quelula" Th*m*s H*rdy says this scenario was thrust upon him by another: "My philosophy of life saves me from sense of responsibility for any of my writings; but I venture to hold myself specially irresponsible for this one."

FRANK HARRIS

Frank Harris (1854–1931), miscellaneous writer and novelist, was Max's first editor on the *Saturday Review* (Beerbohm had but one formal job in his career, that of theatre critic for this journal from 1898 to 1910). Harris was an able editor, a great talker, and, if we are to credit his autobiography, an enormously successful woman-izer. As Max, a friend and one of Harris's "best listeners," put it, "Women like men to be confident, and Frank did not lack confidence." Harris was an egomaniac: "When you believe yourself omnipotent," Max said of him, "it's hard to reconcile yourself to mere potency. Like all deeply arrogant men, Harris possessed little or no sense of reality." An inveterate liar, he told the truth, Max said, only "when his invention flagged." Harris was obsessed with Shakespeare, on whom he wrote and lectured widely (one of his lectures was called "Shakespeare, Shaw, and Frank Harris"). During a large luncheon in 1896 Max heard Harris's voice booming above the din, "like the organ of Westminster Abbey, with infallible footwork." Harris was exclaiming: "Unnatural vice! I know nothing of the joys of unnatural vice. You must ask my friend Oscar Wilde about them. But, had Shakespeare asked me, I should have had to submit." Whereupon Max

xxxi

drew the caricature "Had Shakespeare asked me..."
(Plate 9).

Max's parody of Harris's lengthy *The Man Shakespeare* (1909) nicely captures that work's self-assured,
I'll-clear-up-the-mysteries tone. Harris's book attacks all
other commentators, all the "Professors," whom he sees,
as Carlyle saw other historians, as Dryasdusts producing
"libraries of inanities...conceited dilettantism and
pedantry [and]...prurient stupidity." Having waded
through "tons of talk," Harris finds that "Without a single
exception the commentators have all missed the man
and the story." Goethe and Coleridge, Harris loftily
grants, had some very slight "glimpses" into Shakespeare, but Harris, doing what no one else has attempted,
discovers that Shakespeare "painted himself at full-
length, not once, but twenty times" in his plays and
sonnets. In the latter, for example, Harris sorts out the
whole of Shakespeare's love life, angrily dismissing and
"absolutely" disproving—with quotation followed by
assertion—the slightest hint of homosexual intimacy.
The lines some would read as expressions of homosexual love are "explained by the fact that Shakespeare's
liking for the young Lord Herbert was heightened by
snobbishness and by the hope of patronage"—
snobbishness (in the earlier sense of currying favor with
aristocrats or the wealthy) being one of Shakespeare's
"salient peculiarities." In Max's parody, H*rr*s explains
what he calls Shakespeare's "unconquerable loathing of
Christmas" on the grounds that his wife, Anne Hathaway,
was born on Christmas Day. This is right on target, for
Harris himself is customarily authoritative in discussing
Shakespeare's relationship with his wife: marriage was
the great mistake of Shakespeare's life, although it pro-

pelled him to become what he became. All in all, Harris explains, "Shakespeare's loathing for his wife was measureless, was a part of his own self-esteem." Harris will abide no benign reading of the bit in Shakespeare's will that leaves his "second-best bed" to Anne. No, the poet was bitter to the last, and indeed, even from the grave railed against her: the lines that Shakespeare composed for his own tomb, cursing anyone who disturbs his grave and moves his bones, were written, according to Harris, "in order to prevent his wife being buried with him. He wanted to be free of her in death as in life." Harris is, if anything, more zanily dogmatic than is H*rr*s.

ARNOLD BENNETT

Arnold Bennett (1867–1931), prolific writer of novels and plays, was a self-made, driven man from the Potteries, the six Staffordshire towns amalgamated into Stoke-on-Trent in 1908. Bennett left school at 16 to become a lawyer's clerk; at 21 he went to London where he took up freelance journalism and became the editor of a weekly called *Woman* (his own columns for it were signed "Barbara"). Real success came to him only with his masterpiece, *The Old Wives' Tale* (1908), set chiefly in the "Five Towns," as he called the Potteries. Bennett wrote three more first-rate books, again set in the Five Towns: the Clayhanger Trilogy, comprising *Clayhanger* (1910), *Hilda Lessways* (1911), and *These Twain* (1915). For the rest he wrote humorous books, light fiction, sensation novels, plays, and miscellaneous works, all pretty much unremembered today. But the "Five Towns" books, somber and slow-moving, simply, even repetitiously written, remain a considerable achievement. Margaret Drabble, Bennett's biographer, observes of these books that "Bennett is one of the greatest writers of the passage of time in the English language." In this judgment Max had anticipated her: Henry James, who thought *Hilda Lessways* "like the slow squeezing-out of a big, dirty sponge," informed Max he did not think much of *The Old Wives' Tale* either, asking, "'What's it all about?'... Why, I told him, it's about the passing of time, about the stealthy merging of youth into age, the invisibility of the traps in our own characters into which we walk, unwary, unknowing."

In a few pages of parody Max wouldn't attempt the passage of time; instead, in "Scruts," he focuses on Bennett's Five-Towns setting (Bursley, the fictional equivalent of Burslem), inventing suitable local customs (such as "scruts," chunks of defective pottery added to the Christmas pudding), and dialect (like the greeting "So you're here, are you?"); and, of course, he reincarnates Bennett's style and method, right down to the footnotes referring the reader to other books in the Clayhanger trilogy.

Bennett was especially good at depicting women and their needs and deprivations. Drabble remarks that the second sentence of *Hilda Lessways* sounds as though it came "straight from a modern woman novelist's pen": "Hilda hated domestic work, and because she hated it she often did it passionately and thoroughly." (This same sentence exhibits another tic of Bennett's that Max incorporates, his penchant for the apparently contradictory.) In Max's parody, Emily Wrackgarth, his version of the resolute, stoical Hilda Lessways, is clearly, as the narrator says, "a young woman not to be trifled with."

INTRODUCTION

Like many of Bennett's characters, Emily is much given to introspection:

> She would not try to explain, to reconcile. She abandoned herself to the exquisite mysteries of existence. And yet in her abandonment she kept a sharp look-out for herself, trying fiercely to make head or tail of her nature. She thought herself a fool. But the fact that she thought so was for her a proof of adult sapience. Odd! She gave herself up. And yet it was just by giving herself up that she seemed to glimpse sometimes her own inwardness. And these bleak revelations saddened her. But she savoured her sadness. It was the wine of life to her. And for her sadness she scorned herself, and in her conscious scorn she recovered her self-respect.

One catches here, among other things, Bennett's proclivity for paradoxes, and also for having characters talk to themselves about ultimates and about "life." In *Clayhanger*, for example, Edwin Clayhanger does so continually: showing a young woman through a half-built house, he says to himself, "I haven't known what life *is*! I've been asleep. This is life!" At another time, "He had a tingling consciousness of being unusually alive." Later, "He had amorously kissed a woman. All his past life sank away, and he began a new life." After learning that Hilda Lessways, to whom he had become engaged, is in fact married to another man: "It could be said of Edwin that he fully lived that night." In the aftermath of this devastating revelation, he wakes from sleep "aware of an intensified perception of himself as a physical organism. He thought calmly, '*What a fine thing life is!*'" And in the very last lines of the novel, when Edwin and Hilda finally

INTRODUCTION

decide to join their lives, Edwin "braced himself to the exquisite burden of life." In "Scruts" the somewhat diffident hero Albert Grapp, as he enters Emily's house, muses: "This, he told himself, was life. He, Albert Grapp, was alive. And the world was full of other men, all alive; and yet, because they were not doing Miss Wrackgarth's bidding, none of them really lived. He was filled with a vague melancholy. But his melancholy pleased him."

Many of Bennett's lasting works are melancholy and brooding; they are pessimistic, but with a kind of resignation not altogether sad. "Scruts," lighthearted as it is, somehow captures that tone, captures it without deprecating it—while playing on it that beam of disarming light which Meredith, whom Max so admired, called the Comic Spirit.

JOHN GALSWORTHY

John Galsworthy (1867–1933), novelist and playwright, already famous in 1912 as the author of *The Man of Property*, the first and finest segment of *The Forsyte Saga*, was an admired friend of Max's. The parody of Galsworthy, "Endeavour," written in a carefully observant, somewhat dry style, manifests that admiration for what it mocks—including the fundamental sympathy that can be seen as the key to Galsworthy as a writer and a person. (Beerbohm once described Galsworthy as a "dry man but sympathetic[, who] looks very like his manner of writing." See Plate 11.)

A brief but helpful example of Galsworthy's style and concerns can be gleaned from the story "Comfort"—published in *A Commentary* (1908)—a short piece which some think Max had in mind when writing

INTRODUCTION

"Endeavour" (although, as in most of the parodies, Max is plainly trying to capture the feel and tone of a large body of an author's work rather than to parody a single piece of writing). "Comfort" is a sketch of an upper middle-class couple living comfortably in a fifth-floor London flat:

> It was very pleasant living up so high, where they were not disturbed by noises, scents, or the sight of other people—except such people as themselves. For, quite unconsciously, they had long found out that it was best not to be obliged to see, or hear, or smell anything that made them feel uncomfortable.

Comfort is what these two people seek, at almost all costs. However:

> Every now and then they would come home indignant or distressed, having seen a lost dog, or a horse dead from heat or overwork. They were peculiarly affected by the sufferings of animals; and covering her pink ears, she would cry: "Oh, Dick! how horrible!" or he would say: "Damn! don't rub it in, old girl!" If they had seen any human being in distress, they rarely mentioned, or indeed remembered it, partly because it was such a common sight, partly because their instincts reasoned thus: "If I once begin to see what is happening before my eyes all day and every day, I shall either feel uncomfortable and be compelled to give time and sympathy and money, and do harm into the bargain, destroying people's independence; or I shall become cynical, which is repulsive. But, if I stay in my own garden—as it were—and never look outside, I shall not see what is happening, and if I do not see, it will be as if there were nothing there to see!"

INTRODUCTION

Max's "Endeavour," which seems to contain so much of Galsworthy, is the one parody for which evidence survives of Max commenting directly on it to the parodied author. Writing in late 1912 from London, where he was on a flying visit, Max discusses two questions about the parody that Galsworthy had raised in a letter to him. The first is "scents": "In London my nostrils are conscious of nothing but the smoke and the petrol; and what I wrote about scents in my parody of you was but an expression of envy: it must be lovely to be able to distinguish pretty scents in London. (I myself hardly know which is petrol, which smoke.)" Scents are everywhere in Galsworthy, not only literal scents—as in the quoted passage from "Comfort," but metaphorical ones. In the very first chapter of *The Man of Property* we read that the Forsytes express resentment by means of "the sniff." They scent danger to what they stand for; and when the central figure, Soames Forsyte, is first introduced he is "carrying his nose with that aforesaid appearance of 'sniff,' as though despising an egg which he knew he could not digest." In "Endeavour",

> Adrian Berridge paused on the threshold, as was his wont, with closed eyes and dilated nostrils, enjoying the aroma of complex freshness which the dining-room had at this hour. Pathetically a creature of habit, he liked to savour the various scents, sweet or acrid, that went to symbolise for him the time and the place. Here were the immediate scents of dry toast, of China tea, of napery fresh from the wash, together with that vague, super-subtle scent which boiled eggs give out through their unbroken shells. And as a permanent base to these there was the scent of much-polished

INTRODUCTION

Chippendale, and of bees'-waxed parquet, and of Persian rugs. To-day, moreover, crowning the composition, there was the delicate pungency of the holly that topped the Queen Anne mirror and the Mantegna prints.

The other matter Galsworthy pointed to in the parody is the attitude of mind of those who support various "causes." Galsworthy, a kind of independent Liberal, worked for, wrote about, and gave money to many causes, including divorce law reform, minimum wages, women's suffrage, slum clearance, and prison reform. But more of his energies were spent in campaigns to alleviate animal suffering; he worked for reform of zoos and slaughterhouses; against the misuse of traffic horses and of ponies in mines; against vivisection of animals, dental experiments on animals, and pigeon shooting; he was particularly concerned with the Plumage Bill (against the use of egret plumes for women's hats) and with caged wild birds.

The upper middle-class couple in "Endeavour," Adrian and Jacynth Berridge, keep and virtually worship a pet canary named Amber, but they have ceased to feed wild birds. However, when a starving robin alights on their window-sill, the wife weakens in her resolve:

"Adrian," she faltered, "mightn't we for once—it is Christmas Day—mightn't we, just to-day, sprinkle some bread-crumbs?" ...

At length, "Oh Jacynth," he groaned, "don't—don't tempt me."

"But surely, dear, surely——"

"Jacynth, don't you remember that long talk we had last winter, after the annual meeting of the

Feathered Friends' League,* and how we agreed that
those sporadic doles could do no real good—must
even degrade the birds who received them—and that
we had no right to meddle in what ought to be done
by collective action of the State?"

Minutes later the robin dies, and presently Jacynth says:

"Adrian, are you sure that we, you and I, for all our
theories, and all our efforts, aren't futile?"

"No, dear. Sometimes I am not sure. But—there's
a certain comfort in not being sure. To die for what
one knows to be true, as many saints have done—that
is well. But to live, as many of us do nowadays, in
service of what may, for aught we know, be only a
half-truth or not true at all—this seems to me nobler
still."

"Because it takes more out of us?"

"Because it takes more out of us."

Galsworthy wrote asking about the phrase "Because
it takes more out of us," which apparently spoke his own
thoughts exactly. Max answered, "I think I may claim
that I 'divined' it. I don't think it is in any of your books;
and I don't think you ever said it to me: you would have
adjudged me too frivolous for such a confidence. I must
have read it in your eyes—particularly in the unmonocled
eye!" Galsworthy replied: "You are the nearest approach
to the Yogi that our western civilization produces."

---

* Max's name is no sillier than the actual ones: the Royal Society for
the Protection of Birds, for example, grew out of a small women's
group in Croydon who called themselves the Fur, Fin and Feather
Folk.

INTRODUCTION

G. S. STREET

George Street (1867–1936), journalist and author, wrote
essays, nostalgic books about the eighteenth century,
and one work still read today, *The Autobiography of a
Boy*, a humorous satire on the decadence and dandyism
of the 1890s. Street and Max were very old and very
close friends. David Cecil calls Street "a variation on a
Max theme" in that he was a dandy and a wit, known for
his almost perverse fastidiousness. "I dined the other
night with George Street," Max told a friend, "who was
very much upset because Chesterton, in some article,
had referred to him as 'that brilliant and delightful writer,
Mr G. S. Street.'" For many years Max struggled without
success to get people to read Street's books. And when
Street died Max wrote an appreciation in *The Times* in
which he said that Street, whom he knew well for more
than forty years,

> was of all the men that I have known the most
> exquisitely civilized. I never heard him say ... one
> foolish thing, or a dull thing, or an ill-natured thing, or
> a thing that had not somewhat of the flavour of the
> very best old dry sherry. His wisdom was all the
> kindlier and more lucid from being uncomplicated
> with enthusiasms. ... Intensely literary and (as many
> an equally literary man is not) a born writer, he had
> yet no inclination to set literature above actual things,
> and preferred the passing pageant of life.

After reading that encomium one comes to Street's essays
with high expectations. Street pleasantly worries a subject, goes round and round it; meanders, strays from the
point, and freely, informally admits doing so—with a

phrase such as "but that is by the way." A typical Street essay, "Of Inferior People," opens:

> It is all very well to denounce superior people, but I am inclined to think that inferior people are, on the whole, a more serious inconvenience.
> By the way, I am not denouncing the whole human race. I may look as though I am at first sight, because no one is really quite the average; we are all superior or inferior in one sense. But this is a foolish quibble, not worth explaining: we must keep strictly to business.

Street sometimes overuses the first person pronoun; he loves strained negatives; he indulges occasionally in deliberately struggling syntax—"Fitly to describe any visible thing whatever is the work of an artist, I question not." He is fond of short sentences and phrases: "Very good," "Oh dear! oh dear," "Alas." (Street's essay "The Plague of Newspapers" ends with the word "Alas," as does Max's parody.)
Street's frequent themes involve manners, snobbishness, vulgarity, the rich, motor cars, Bond Street, the evils of the twentieth century compared to the "careful sanity and justice of the eighteenth." Everything is put forth by way of a complaint. In the essay "Waiting for Dinner" Street says of people who keep one waiting in a restaurant by arriving forty-five minutes late:

> It is almost incredible, but true, that there are men and women so destitute of imagination that they rea-lise nothing of the suffering they cause, and honestly think their offence a light one: they prove it by offering frankly a trivial excuse. I can only say that

INTRODUCTION

they are unfit for civilised life.... So wonderful is human conceit that these criminals often seem to suppose that they are popular people at the very moment of their crime. They enter smiling, tell a glib lie, or say that are so sorry with obvious unconcern. The fatuous fools!

Street's grievances are set forth in strong language, intended humorously: many of his acquaintances are "great bloated blockheads" and "fat-headed moralists"; all editors are "brutes"; the Man of Business "belongs to the stupidest portion of a stupid race.... Kick him off his pedestal"; doctors are "humbugs" and "the whole medical profession reeks of its origin" in the medicine man, which is fine because today's patients are "practically savages in their mental constitution." An essay named "Our Food and Drink" begins, "It is really a wonder we survive," and goes on to call the wine merchant "a murderer on a large scale":

> What is to be done? The Government is of no use, purveyors of drink are incurably homicidal, and my fellow-drinkers are too hopelessly rabbit-brained to combine against this murderous injustice. I suppose I must go on slowly being done to death.

In the essay "Other People's Manners" we read:

> No doubt about it; new occasions demand new codes of manners, when natural kindness is not sufficient for guidance without them. Motors have shown this distressing fact, and golf and bridge. And by the way, Turkish baths. A special code should be drawn for Turkish bathers.... Absolute silence in the hottest rooms, please, so that languorous poetry may lightly

fan our brains; how can it when two dullards are argu-
ing about a stupid play; and kindly kill that gentleman
who is scolding an attendant.

Street's essays are today as little remembered as
Benson's. Even when one grants that the casual essay
seldom has a long life, these are disappointing. For the
most part they are not very funny. Their affected anger is
not convincing, and the overall tone is one of grumpiness.
Nor does much thought lie behind the bantering tone.
Max's parody "Christmas" captures everything, from the
annoyance and the wandering focus, to the pet themes—
the superiority of the eighteenth century to the twentieth
century, breeding, manners, vulgarity, the rich, motor
cars, the excellence of Trollope. Of Bond Street window
displays, Str**t says, "This sort of thing lashes me to
ungovernable fury. The lion is roused, and I recognise in
myself a born leader of men. Be so good as to smash those
windows for me"—hardly an exaggeration of "kindly kill
that gentleman who is scolding an attendant." But, perhaps perforce, the parody too is a little disappointing. To
see the rare kind of essay that survives one must turn
from Street's to Max's own. One strong recommendation
to do so comes from Virginia Woolf, who wrote to him in
1928: "If you knew how I had pored over your essays—
how they fill me with marvel—how I can't conceive what
it would be like to write as you do!"

JOSEPH CONRAD

Max's imitation of Joseph Conrad (1857–1924) is sound
evidence of parody as criticism. It is worth noting that
two standard collections of Conrad criticism begin by

reprinting "The Feast." The editor of one of these collections, Marvin Mudrick, says of Conrad's early melodramatic short story "The Lagoon" that it "is as ludicrous
as Max Beerbohm's parody of it; it pours out cataracts of
the silliest and most narcissistic prose by any major
writer in English." (Mudrick supports his assertion by
quoting sentences such as "The ever-ready suspicion of
evil, the gnawing suspicion that lurks in our hearts,
flowed out into the stillness round him—into the stillness profound and dumb, and made it appear untrust-
worthy and infamous, like the placid and impenetrable
mask of an unjustifiable violence.")

"The Feast" does seem to draw on "The Lagoon."
Conrad's story opens:

> The white man, lean[ed] with both arms over the roof
> of the little house in the stern of the boat. . . . At the
> end of the straight avenue of forests cut by the in-
> tense glitter of the river, the sun appeared unclouded
> and dazzling, poised low over the water that shone
> like a band of metal. The forests, sombre and dull,
> stood motionless and silent on each side of the broad
> stream. At the foot of big, towering trees, trunkless
> nipa palms rose from the mud of the bank, in bunches
> of leaves enormous and heavy, that hung unstirring
> over the brown swirl of eddies. In the stillness of the
> air every tree, every leaf, every bough, every tendril of
> creeper and every petal of minute blossoms seemed
> to have been bewitched into an immobility perfect
> and final.

"The Feast" begins:

> The hut in which slept the white man was on a
> clearing between the forest and the river. Silence, the

INTRODUCTION

silence murmurous and unquiet of a tropical night, brooded over the hut that, baked through by the sun, sweated a vapour beneath the cynical light of the stars. . . . The roofs of the congested trees, writhing in some kind of agony private and eternal, made tenebrous and shifty silhouettes against the sky, like shapes cut out of black paper by a maniac who pushes them with his thumb this way and that, irritably, on a concave surface of blue steel. Resin oozed unseen from the upper branches to the trunks swathed in creepers that clutched and interlocked with tendrils venomous, frantic and faint.

Conrad himself, for whom public acceptance had come slowly, wrote in 1923 of "The Lagoon": "I have lived long enough to see it most agreeably guyed by Mr Max Beerbohm in a volume of parodies entitled 'A Christmas Garland,' where I found myself in very good company. I was immensely gratified. I began to believe in my public existence." Actually, a more careful look at Max's parody shows that it distills elements from much of Conrad's early fiction, including *Almayer's Folly*, *An Outcast of the Islands*, "Karain," and *Heart of Darkness*. And, as Addison C. Bross has shown, "The Feast" draws especially upon another story, "An Outpost of Progress," considered one of Conrad's finest short fictions, and a kind of companion piece to the renowned *Heart of Darkness*. "An Outpost" has a generous share of Conradian rhetorical flourishes, including the frequent postpositioning of adjectives, and that special tone suggestive of vague, mysterious, often atmospheric, evil: "The day had come, and a heavy mist had descended on the land: the mist penetrating, enveloping, and silent; the morning

xlvi

INTRODUCTION

mist of tropical lands; the mist that clings and kills; the mist white and deadly, immaculate and poisonous"; "After a few moments of an agony frightful and absurd, he decided to go and meet his doom"; "A shriek inhuman, vibrating and sudden, pierced like a sharp dart the white shroud of that land of sorrow."

"An Outpost" also exemplifies situations and character types prominent in Conrad's early fiction and spoofed in the Beerbohm parody. Central in this respect is a dense, self-important white man, a commercial adventurer, a representative of western civilization, who is out-witted by a clever, cunning native. In "An Outpost" the white world is represented by two obtuse traders, Kayerts and Carlier, and they are outsmarted by Makola, a native who sells their black working-men into slavery. The two whites eventually die: Kayerts shoots Carlier—after the crazed pair have a falling-out over whether "just once" to use their dwindling sugar supply in the coffee—and then hangs himself. Kayerts is "short and fat"; in "The Feast" Mr Williams, the white trader, is "corpulent and pale"; Makola's corresponding native character is named Mahamo—an obvious echo—and he sells Williams himself to cannibals who will make a "feast" of him.

Throughout the parody there is play upon the notion of illusion, so central in Conrad. Again, "An Outpost" offers characteristic examples. The narrator muses how most people know next to nothing about oppression, cruelty, devotion, or virtue: "Nobody knows what suffering or sacrifice mean—except, perhaps, the victims of the mysterious purpose of these illusions." While Kayerts and Carlier are engaged in their mortal struggle, Kayerts wonders how they could have quarrelled so

INTRODUCTION

fatally over sugar for their coffee: he "thought it must be a horrible illusion." In "The Feast," in Mahamo's "upturned eyes, and along the polished surface of his lean body black and immobile, the stars were reflected, creating an illusion of themselves who are illusions"; Mr Williams "was covered with a mosquito-net that was itself illusory like everything else, only more so"; and at the end, when Williams is running amid a shower of spears, he thinks his death would be a "grave loss to his employers. This . . . was an illusion. It was the last of Mr Williams' illusions."

Some people returning to Conrad after reading "The Feast" will find much of his prose style and many of his themes, and certainly the word *illusion*, freighted with the impish cargo the parody brings to them.

EDMUND GOSSE

Edmund Gosse (1849–1928) was a man who revelled in the literary life: he published nearly a hundred books; he engaged in countless literary friendships; he fostered younger writers (see Plate 15). This he did while working for a living as a cataloguer in the British Museum, then as a translator for the Board of Trade, and finally as librarian of the House of Lords. Gosse knew everybody who wrote books. In 1920 his literary friends—including Max—presented him with a bust of himself for his seventieth birthday. (See Max's caricature, Plate 22, of Gosse assuring a tearful George Moore that "of *course*" they will give him a bust too, but he must tell them when his seventieth birthday is.) In 1925 Gosse was knighted for his contributions to literature. Today he is remem-

xlviii

INTRODUCTION

bered solely for his masterpiece, *Father and Son*, an autobiographical account of his childhood and youth with a fanatically Calvinistic parent. Much of his other writing was biographical—"the history of authors"—and he wrote full-length studies of John Donne, Coventry Patmore, Ibsen, Swinburne, and his own father, together with numerous shorter lives. In his brief biographical sketches he practiced what he called "anecdotal history," drawing "faithfully from the life," and he did so with a flair for the catching (sometimes purple) phrase, and the pose of himself as an innocent go-between among the famous. He apparently threw these anecdotal portraits together with what Henry James—a staunch friend—called his "genius for inaccuracy." (See Ann Thwaite's biography of Gosse for a lively account of the scandal that arose when Gosse, while Clark Lecturer at Cambridge, published his lectures as *From Shakespeare to Pope*, and brought upon himself an attack from one John Churton Collins, who accused him of everything from "habitual inaccuracy with respect to dates" and an "ignorance of the simplest facts and dates of Literature and History"—like thinking Sidney's *Arcadia* was a poem—to all sorts of "absurdities in criticism and such vices of style as will in the eyes of the discerning reader carry with them their own condemnation." Collins's strictures were by and large valid, but the literary world, including friends like Tennyson, Browning, Meredith, James, Hardy, and Swinburne closed ranks round one of their own. "Correct a date or two in the second edition" was their advice. However, Gosse's reputation was thereafter somewhat damaged, and for a time to commit a howler was "to make a Gosse of oneself." In 1891 William Archer attacked him for inept translations of

INTRODUCTION

Ibsen, giving as evidence Gosse's rendering of a passage
Archer knew was meant to mean "distinguished himself
on the battlefield" as "always voted right at elections.")

Gosse, since 1872, had distinguished himself as the
introducer of Ibsen to the English-speaking world. He
did not meet the great man himself until 1899, and Max's
notion of having Gosse two decades earlier introduce
the famous Norwegian playwright to Browning—whom
Gosse did know well—was purely fictitious, and, as it
turned out, inspired. By way of background, here are a
few lines from Gosse on Browning:

> Of all great poets, except (one fancies) Chaucer, he
> must have been the most accessible. It is almost
> a necessity with imaginative genius of a very high
> order to require support from without: sympathy,
> admiration, amusement, must be constantly poured in
> to balance the creative evaporation. But Mr Browning
> demanded no such tribute. He rather hastened for-
> ward with both hands full of entertainment for the
> new-comer, anxious to please rather than hoping to
> be pleased. The most part of men of genius look upon
> an unknown comer as certainly a bore and probably
> an enemy, but to Robert Browning the whole world
> was full of vague possibilities of friendship. . . . In this
> close of our troubled century . . . the robust health of
> Robert Browning's mind and body has presented a
> singular and a most encouraging phenomenon. He
> missed the morbid over-refinement of the age; the
> processes of his mind were sometimes even a little
> coarse, and always delightfully direct. . . . The vibra-
> tion of his loud voice, his hard fist upon the table,
> would make very short work with cobwebs. But this
> external roughness, like the rind of a fruit, merely

served to keep the inner sensibilities young and fresh. None of his instincts grew old.... The subtlest of writers, he was the simplest of men.

In Max's parody this simplest of men is introduced, through Gosse's agency, to the far less simple Ibsen. The account is full of the concrete and illuminating detail Gosse used in his portraits: the time is set forth in a phrase typical of Gosse, "In the third week of December, 1878" (though Gosse often got his dates wrong, the specifics conveyed an air of authenticity); Browning is placed solidly in his Palazzo Rezzonico at Venice, "The yellow haze of a wintry Venetian sunshine poured in through the vast windows of his *salone*, making an aureole around his silvered head." Ibsen is discovered accidentally in the Piazza San Marco: "My thoughts of Browning were all of a sudden scattered by the vision of a small, thick-set man seated at one of the tables in the Café Florian. This was—and my heart leapt like a young trout when I saw that it could be none other than— Henrik Ibsen." Neither man has heard of the other, and their meeting for Christmas turkey and plum pudding (readers of *Father and Son* will recall the significance of Christmas plum pudding in that work) veers on catastrophe. After the parody was published in 1912 in *A Christmas Garland*, Gosse, telling Max how Henry James liked the book, went on to underscore James's point that no one could now write without incurring the reproach of imitating Max: "And, alas! my dear Max, what can be more true? I, for instance, shall never be able to draw another portrait without calling down upon me the sneer, 'Not half so amusing as your dinner with Ibsen and Browning!' You are our Conqueror. And I am your affectionate and ever-amused admirer." Max, who labored painfully over most of his writing (though he drew caricatures swiftly and with pleasure) is on record as saying, "The only things I ever wrote with joy—easily—were ' "Savonarola" Brown' [in *Seven Men*] and the meeting between Ibsen and Browning in *A Christmas Garland*."

HILAIRE BELLOC

Of Hilaire Belloc (1870–1953), Max said, "He had the conviction that there was only a single lane to Heaven." Or, as he put it another time, "Of course, I can only speak for man; but Mr. Belloc knows God's point of view." Belloc, a man of partly French parentage and combative religious (Roman Catholic) and social (liberal) opinions, was yet another writer who turned out over a hundred books (of which *The Path to Rome*, 1902, was the most famous). He celebrated, and even bottled, wine; was enamoured of everything French, and loved travel—especially in the French countryside. He had a marvellously mannered, accretive prose style, a frank, friendly, sporting, good-natured, informal button-holing of the reader, in the midst of airy philosophizing, wide-ranging references to places and people—preferably French—anecdotes galore, Latin tags, pronouncements as if from on high, a clearing-up of errors, and a proclivity for spending most of his effort on something other than his announced central point, and for asserting victory in debate rather than attempting to argue his case.

A typical Belloc essay, "On the Approach of an Awful Doom," from *On Nothing* (1908), proceeds like this:

lii

INTRODUCTION

The time has come to convey, impart and make
known to you the dreadful conclusions and horrible
prognostications that flow, happen, deduce, derive
and are drawn from the truly abominable conditions
of the social medium in which you and I and all poor
devils are most fatally and surely bound to draw out
our miserable existence.

There follows, not an examination of the announced
subject, but an exploration of "existence" versus "ex-
istences." This discussion, after a peripheral, glancing
dismissal of Rousseau ("a fig for the Genevese!") and
Hobbes ("the mind of a lame, halting and ill-furnished
clockmaker, and a blight on him!"), goes forward:

> It is a very pretty question and would have been ex-
> cellently debated by Thomas Aquinas in the Jacobins
> of St. Jacques, near the Parloir aux Bourgeois, by the
> gate of the University; by Albertus Magnus in the
> Cordeliers, hard by the college of Bourgoyne; by Pico
> de la Mirandole who lived I care not a rap where and
> debated I know not from Adam how or when; by Lord
> Bacon, who took more bribes in a day than you and I
> could compass in a dozen years; by Spinoza, a good
> worker of glass lenses, but a philosopher whom I
> have never read nor will; by Coleridge when he was
> not talking about himself or taking some filthy drug;
> by John Pilkington Smith, of Norwood, Drysalter,
> who has, I hear, been lately horribly bitten by the
> metaphysic; and by a crowd of others.

Belloc then announces, "But that's all by the way,"
although the existence/existences theme won't go away,
and Seven Questions are put—in Latin—and it is back to
"this most important and necessary [question]—namely,

INTRODUCTION

whether real existence can be predicated of matter." We
are informed that "Anaxagoras of Syracuse, that was
tutor to the Tyrant Machion, being in search upon this
question for a matter of seventy-two years, four months,
three days and a few odd hours and minutes, did, in
extreme old age, as he was walking by the shore at the
sea, hit, as it were in a flash, upon six of the seven
answers." But his failure to pronounce on that last
question "*sive an non* (that is, whether it *were* real or
no)" leaves the whole business undecided to this day.
"So there we are and an answer must be found, but upon
my soul I forget to what it hangs, though I know well
there was some question propounded at the beginning of
this for which I cared a trifle at the time of asking it and
you I hope not at all." Next, with time for "one bout"
more, Belloc discourses on *de gustibus*— "I say live and
let live"—and at last recalls that his subject might have
touched on capital and the rich swallowing everyone
up, but as it won't happen, according to contemporary
prophets, for thirty years, "why then let us make the best
of the time we have, and sail, ride, travel, write, drink,
sing and all be friends together; and do you go about
doing good to the utmost of your power, as I heartily
hope you will, though from your faces I doubt it hugely.
A blessing I wish you all."

Max's parody, "Of Christmas," captures all this, and
includes additionally a Belloc-like essay-starting anec-
dote that begins with a long sentence, halfway through
which many of Belloc's stylistic and mental mannerisms
are unmistakable:

There was a man came to an Inn by night, and after he
had called three times they should open him the

door—though why three times, and not three times three, nor thirty times thirty, which is the number of the little stone devils that make mows at St Aloesius of Ledera over against the marshes Gué-la-Nuce to this day, nor three hundred times three hundred (which is a bestial number), nor three thousand times three-and-thirty, upon my soul I know not, and nor do you—when, then, this jolly fellow had three times cried out, shouted, yelled, holloa'd, loudly besought, caterwauled, brayed, sung out, and roared, he did by the same token set himself to beat, hammer, bang, pummel, and knock at the door.

Eventually the traveller, "Trot" Dimby, is dismissed for a look at "that One Great Ultimate and Final True Thing" that B*ll*c wants to say about Christmas. But first he must "curse, gibbet, and denounce *in execrationem perpetuam atque æternam*" those who seek Truth in a crafty and calculating way rather than going "blindly at it" in the "honest fashion of men." He next bursts into verse—"there is nothing like verse to clear the mind"*— lines he will sing at dawn tomorrow on the high green

---

* Belloc had a special talent for light verse, much of it in praise of Jesus, the Virgin Mary, wine, or beer. Typical is the "West Sussex Drinking Song" from *Verses* (1910):

> They sell good Beer at Haslemere
>   And under Guildford Hill.
> At Little Cowfold as I've been told
>   A beggar may drink his fill:
> There is good brew in Amberley too,
>   And by the bridge also;
> But the swipes they take in at Washington Inn
>   Is the very best Beer I know.

barrow at Storrington ("where the bones of Athelstan's men are"):

> The floods are out and the ford is narrow,
> The stars hang dead and my limbs are lead,
>   But ale is gold
>   And there's good foot-hold
> On the Cuckfield side of Storrington Barrow.

"Such then, as I see it, is the whole pith, mystery, outer form, common acceptation, purpose, usage usual, meaning and inner meaning, beauty intrinsic and extrinsic, and right character of Christmas Feast.... Pray for my soul."

What Max especially admired in Belloc's writing, in which he found "splendid things abounding" in the midst of "a lot of absolute chaotic rot," was an "enormous gusto."

G. B. SHAW

Towards George Bernard Shaw (1856–1950) Max felt, though without the animus, as he did towards Kipling: here was genius wasted. The two men were on friendly, joking terms. When in 1903 Shaw wrote to Max, disputing his review of *Man and Superman*, Max wrote back saying he would preserve and treasure Shaw's letter for its "engaging sophistries." Half a century later Max still maintained that Shaw had been "talking rot" all that time: "Will anyone ever write a book on the vast amount of nonsense uttered with such brilliance and panache by G. B. S.?"

In "A Straight Talk" Max parodies Shaw's prefaces

INTRODUCTION

that so cleverly combine braggadocio with humility.
Typical is the preface to *The Devil's Disciple*, the section
"On Diabolonian Ethics," in which Shaw, defending
the practice of writing prefaces, calls himself a first-
class critic and philosopher, and also a charlatan and
mountebank. Most playwrights, he says, don't furnish
their plays with prefaces because they can't write them.
But Shaw won't call in a critic to do the job:

> Now what I say is, why should I get another man to
> praise me when I can praise myself? I have no dis-
> abilities to plead: produce me your best critic, and I
> will criticize his head off. As to philosophy, I taught
> my critics the little they know in my Quintessence of
> Ibsenism; and now they train their guns—the guns I
> gave them—on me, and proclaim that I write as if
> mankind had intellect without will, or heart, as they
> call it. . . . Again they tell me that So and So, who does
> not write prefaces, is no charlatan. Well, I am. I first
> caught the ear of the British public on a cart in Hyde
> Park, to the blaring of brass bands, and this not at all
> as a reluctant sacrifice of my instinct of privacy to
> political necessity, but because, like all dramatists
> and mimes of genuine vocation, I am a natural-born
> mountebank.

But the Shaw preface Max had chiefly in mind seems
to have been the Epistle Dedicatory (addressed to drama
critic A. B. Walkley) of *Man and Superman*. At the time
he wrote the parody—1906—Max considered *Man and
Superman* Shaw's best play; as he told Shaw, while he
thought the play itself very flawed, he judged the inter-
mezzo, the hell scene, the Revolutionist's Handbook, and
the preface almost as good as they could be. The parody

focuses on various Shavian concerns from the preface, most notably originality in literature. Shaw says, "I should make formal acknowledgment to the authors whom I have pillaged in the following pages if I can recollect them all." They include Arthur Conan Doyle, Wells, J. M. Barrie, "a certain West Indian colonial secretary," Sidney Webb, Mozart, William Poel, Bunyan, Blake, Hogarth, Turner, Goethe, Shelley, Schopenhauer, Wagner, Ibsen, Morris, Tolstoy, and Nietzsche. Sh*w says briefly: "Flatly, I stole this play." He explains that it wasn't from lack of ideas, but from laziness: "The reason lies in that bland, unalterable resolve to shirk honest work, by which you recognise the artist as surely as you recognise the leopard by his spots. In so far as I am an artist I am a loafer." Shaw discusses the failings of his most famous English predecessors, Dickens and Shakespeare:

> I read Dickens and Shakespear without shame or stint; but their pregnant observations and demonstrations of life are not co-ordinated into any philosophy or religion: on the contrary, Dickens's sentimental assumptions are violently contradicted by his observations; and Shakespear's pessimism is only his wounded humanity. Both have the specific genius of the fictionist and the common sympathies of human feeling and thought in pre-eminent degree.... But they are concerned with the diversities of the world instead of with its unities.... they have no constructive ideas; they regard those who have them as dangerous fanatics; in all their fictions there is no leading thought or inspiration for which any man could conceivably risk the spoiling of his hat in a

shower, much less his life. Both are alike forced
to borrow motives for the more strenuous actions
of their personages from the common stockpot of
melodramatic plots. . . . The truth is, the world was to
Shakespear a great "stage of fools" on which he was
utterly bewildered. He could see no sort of sense in
living at all; and Dickens saved himself from the
despair of the dream in The Chimes by taking the
world for granted and busying himself with its details.
Neither of them could do anything with a serious
positive character.

And so on at very great length. In "A Straight Talk" the
entire discussion consists of the following:

Charles Dickens had lucid intervals in which he was
vaguely conscious of the abuses around him; but his
spasmodic efforts to expose these brought him into
contact with realities so agonising to his highstrung
literary nerves that he invariably sank back into
debauches of unsocial optimism. Even the Swan of
Avon had his glimpses of the havoc of displacement
wrought by Elizabethan romanticism in the social
machine which had been working with tolerable
smoothness under the prosaic guidance of Henry 8.
The time was out of joint; and the Swan, recognising
that he was the last person to ever set it right,
consoled himself by offering the world a soothing
doctrine of despair. Not for me, thank you, that
Swansdown pillow. I refuse as flatly to fuddle myself
in the shop of "W. Shakespeare, Druggist," as to
stimulate myself with the juicy joints of "C. Dickens,
Family Butcher." Of these and suchlike pernicious
establishments my patronage consists in weaving

round the shop-door a barbed-wire entanglement of dialectic and then training my moral machine-guns on the customers.

Throughout, Max gets to Shaw's combination of mock humility used as a weapon coupled with a supposedly ironic vanity and arrogance. To Walkley (and the world) Shaw says:

> You must take me as I am, a reasonable, patient, consistent, apologetic, laborious person, with the temperament of a school-master and the pursuits of a vestry-man. No doubt that literary knack of mine which happens to amuse the British public distracts attention from my character; but the character is there none the less, solid as bricks. I have a conscience; and conscience is always anxiously explanatory.

Sh*w says that the many pleasing aesthetic qualities in this "stolen" play belong to the original author, but he adds, "To me the play owes nothing but the stiffening of civistic conscience that has been crammed in. Modest? Not a bit of it. It is my civistic conscience that makes a man of me and (incidentally) makes this play a masterpiece."

When a *Festschrift* was being prepared for Shaw's ninetieth birthday, Max declined to contribute an essay, telling the editor: "Very fond though I am of G. B. S., and immensely kind though he has always been to me, my admiration for his genius has during fifty years and more been marred for me by dissent from almost any view that he holds about anything."

INTRODUCTION

Maurice Hewlett

Maurice Hewlett (1861–1923), novelist, poet, and essayist, is completely forgotten today. Max knew him: "[Hewlett's] flashing eye, his soldierly abruptness, and the mild foolishness of what he says, are always a joy." Of his writings Max gave this estimate in 1906 (the same year he wrote the parody):

> The fascination of his books has always seemed to me rather like the fascination of the theatre—the fascination of a thing which, though it appears so very real, one knows to be not real at all.... [Hewlett] has a passionate clarity of vision. He sees his characters steadily, brilliantly, from top to toe.... And he makes us partakers of his vision. In the round we see them, these fair ladies and their gallants, these proud virgins and generous wantons, these knights with clanking harness and beetling brows. We visualize them as distinctly as we visualize the people who pass us in the street.... But is there life inside them? They are always violent. They express, very picturesquely and delightfully, all the symptoms of love, hatred, despair, political ambition, religious fervour, and what not. They are very eloquent. There is nothing they cannot express. And they flourish their arms, they stride, strut, lurk behind arrases, scale walls, stab themselves, die, exactly as people do in real life, or would do, if they had the chance, and the necessary technique. But somehow, to me at least, they do not seem to be real.... For sheer artistry in the use of words, Mr Hewlett's beats anyone since Robert Louis Stevenson—or Walter Pater.... [Hewlett's style] is

rather too steadily dazzling.... Such conscious and obvious artistry in the use of words is not, I confess, conducive to illusion in the characters presented.... In Mr Hewlett's novels not even Mr Hewlett himself lives vividly for us. We do not see him, we do not know him, behind those glittering arrangements.

And late in life, in his Cambridge Rede Lecture (1943) Max said, "I have always regretted that Maurice Hewlett, one of the lights of the 'nineties and of later years, was not a humourist and wished [instead] to illude us with his tales; for his preciosity was fatal to his wish. Besides, it was a robust preciosity; and that is unnatural, is a contradiction in terms."

The Forest Lovers (1898) Hewlett's most famous work, is described in Albert Baugh's *A Literary History of England* as "an unusual combination of romance, erudition, artifice, and modernism.... a medieval tale avowedly modelled on Malory but too softly voluptuous to remind many readers of its prototype." The story is filled with brave knights, evil knights, mysteries, and mistaken identities. Here is the opening of *The Forest Lovers*:

Prosper Le Gai Rides Out

My story will take you into times and spaces alike rude and uncivil. Blood will be spilt, virgins suffer distresses; the horn will sound through woodland glades; dogs, wolves, deer, and men, Beauty and the Beasts, will tumble each other, seeking life or death with their proper tools. There should be mad work, not devoid of entertainment. When you read the word *Explicit* ["It is explained," or unravelled, the word found at the close of the novel], if you have laboured

so far, you will know something of the Morgraunt
Forest and the Countess Isabel; the Abbot of Holy
Thorn will have postured and schemed (with you
behind the arras); you will have wandered with Isoult
and will know why she was called La Desirous, with
Prosper le Gai, and will understand how a man may
fall in love with his own wife. Finally, of Galors
and his affairs, of the great difference there may be
between a Christian and the brutes, of love and hate,
grudging and open humour, faith and works, cloisters
and thoughts uncloistered—all in a green wood—you
will know as much as I do if you have cared to follow
the argument. I hope you will not ask me what it all
means, or what the moral of it is. I rank myself with
the historian in this business of tale-telling, and
consider that my sole affair is to hunt the argument
dispassionately. Your romancer must be neither a
lover of his heroine nor (as the fashion now sets) of
his chief rascal. . . . He must affect a genial height, that
of a jigger of strings; and his attitude should be that of
the Pulpiteer:—Heaven help you, gentlemen, but I
know what is best for you! Leave everything to me.

Max's parody, "Fond Hearts Askew," placed not in
a medieval forest but the West End theatre district,
exhibits much of the same, including, notably, mistaken
identities and cross-dressing. It's great fun, and very
much Hewlett, except for its welcome brevity.

GEORGE MOORE

George Moore (1852–1933), who came from a well-to-do
Irish family, the Moores of Moore Park, Co. Mayo (they

claimed descent from St Thomas More) was once very
well known, and considered the English Zola. He was the
author of *A Modern Lover, A Mummer's Wife, Esther
Waters*, other novels, plays, essays, and as Max put it,
"many autobiographies."

The essay "Dickens" reflects in its few pages much of
what Max found so intriguing in his friend Moore: the
enthusiasms, the meandering thought, the lack of logic,
the factual gaffes, the constant and frank admiration of
women, the all-absorbing love of things French (something picked up during a decade-long residence in
Paris in his twenties), his championing of the French
Impressionist painters, the innocent, uninstructed, un-
selfconscious appropriation of other writers' material,
the disillusionment with the Irish language as a vehicle
for literature. Max made his parody of Moore a critical
essay because he thought Moore's real genius was as a
critic, not as a novelist. Moore's criticism had, Max
wrote, a "vital magic":

> No one but Ruskin has written more vividly than he,
> more lovingly and seeingly, about the art of painting;
> and no one has ever written more inspiringly than
> he, with a more infectious enthusiasm, about those
> writers whom he understood and loved, or more
> amusingly against those whom he neither understood
> nor liked.

Moore's shifting artistic enthusiasms came partly from
the fact that he seemed to have no past learning; that
"for him, everything was discovery" (Oscar Wilde said
that Moore was "always conducting his education in
public"). Accordingly:

INTRODUCTION

Whenever he discovered some new old master, that
master seemed to him greater than any other: he
would hear of no other. And it was just this frantic
exclusiveness that made his adorations so fruitful: it
was by the completeness of his surrender to one thing
at a time that he possessed himself of that thing's very
essence. The finest criticism is always passive, not
active. . . . I do not mean that he was always faithless
to old idols. When he had exhausted his ecstasy at
some new shrine, he would rise from his knees and, if
no other new shrine were visible, would wander back
to some old one. Turgéneff, especially, had the power
to recapture and re-inflame him ever.

"Dickens" is largely a parody of Moore's manner
in *Confessions of a Young Man* (1888, with various
later revisions), than which it is really very little more
eccentric. Opening the *Confessions* almost at random
one comes on sentences like "I can lay no claim to
scholarship of any kind; for save life I could never learn
anything correctly. I am a student only of ball-rooms,
bar-rooms, streets, and alcoves. I have read very little,
but all I read I can turn to account, and all I read
I remember." Or, "I did not go to either Oxford or
Cambridge, but I went to the Nouvelle Athènes [a Paris
café]." Or, "Education should be confined to clerks, and
it drives even them to drink. Will the world never learn
that we never learn anything that we did not know
before?" His violent likes and dislikes are everywhere,
including the "two dominant notes" in his character,
"an original hatred of my native country, and a brutal
loathing for the religion I was brought up in. All the
aspects of my native country are violently disagreeable

lxv

to me, and I cannot think of the place I was born in without a sensation akin to nausea." As for his personal philosophy:

> That I may die childless—that when my hour comes I may turn my face to the wall saying, I have not increased the great evil of human life—then, though I were murderer, fornicator, thief, and liar, my sins shall melt even as a cloud. But he who dies with children about him, though his life were in all else an excellent deed, shall be held accursed by the truly wise, and the stain upon him shall endure for ever.

As for Art, it was, he said, "individuality": "It does not matter how badly you paint, so long as you don't paint badly like other people." A typical literary judgment: Gustave Kahn's *Les Palais nomades* is a "really beautiful book. For in the first place it is free from those pests and parasites of artistic work—ideas.... Gustave Kahn took counsel of the past, and he has successfully avoided everything that even a hostile critic might be tempted to term an idea; and for this I am grateful." Or consider this brief, complete paragraph: "In youth the genius of Shelley astonished me; but now I find the stupidity of the ordinary person infinitely more surprising."

Compare these with the parody which begins, not of course with Dickens, but with "I had often wondered why when people talked to me of Tintoretto I always found myself thinking of Turgéneff . . . for at first sight nothing can be more far apart than the Slav mind and the Flemish." Arriving at his subject, he asserts boldly, "There never was a writer except Dickens"—even though, distracted by his worship of Balzac, Zola, Yeats, *et tous ces autres*, he has as yet read only the Christmas-

INTRODUCTION

party chapter of *Pickwick Papers*: "Christmas—I see it
now—is the only moment in which men and women are
really alive, are really worth writing about. At other
seasons they do not exist for the purpose of art. I spit on
all seasons except Christmas."

And Dickens's Mr Wardell is "better than all Balzac's
figures rolled into one.... Balzac wrote many books....
One knows that he used to write for fifteen hours at a
stretch, gulping down coffee all the while. But it does not
follow that the coffee was good, nor does it follow that
what he wrote was good. The Comédie Humaine is all
chicory." But the discussion of Dickens's Christmas
chapter inevitably becomes a flight of fancy about
Arabella: for one thing, "only Manet could have stated
the slope of the thighs of the girl"; and presently,
"Strange thoughts of her surge up vaguely in me as I
watch her—thoughts that I cannot express in English....
Elle est plus vieille que les roches...." The next seven
lines in French are lifted word for word from Pater
(another Moore enthusiasm), the famous lines about
the Mona Lisa from his *Renaissance Studies*. But the
plagiarized apotheosis is interrupted by the exclamation
that he cannot express his thoughts even in French
because, like all European languages, French is a "stale
language" ("The stalest of them all is Erse"), everything
followed by the sudden decision to go to Mexico, "buy a
Mexican grammar," and there await the new artistic
dawn. Max loved in Moore his

matchless honesty of mind; his very real modesty
about his own work; his utter freedom from jealousy;
his loving reverence of all that in all arts was nobly
done; and, above all, that inexhaustible patience of

his, and courage, whereby he made the very most of the gifts he had, and earned for himself a gift which Nature had not bestowed on him: the specific gift of *writing*. No young man . . . ever wrote worse than young Moore wrote. It must have seemed to every one that here was a writer who, however interesting he in himself might be, never would learn to express himself tolerably. . . . Some of the good writers have begun with a scant gift for writing. But which of them with no gift at all? Moore is the only instance I ever heard of. Somehow, in the course of long years, he learned to express himself beautifully. I call that great.

The parody, for all its outrageousness, bespeaks its author's love for George Moore. I suspect the "Dickens" may have been Max's own favorite among the parodies.

GEORGE MEREDITH

Max had an extravagant regard for the novels of George Meredith (1828–1909), or at least for the earlier novels. He loved *The Adventures of Harry Richmond* (1871) even more on rereading it in 1920, but found that *Diana of the Crossways* (1885) didn't wear well: "tedious, crack-jaw, arid intellectual snobbery. . . . Diana is as dead as a door-nail, and I tremble to think what the *Amazing Marriage* and *Lord Ormont* [Meredith's last two novels] must be as dead as." But the earlier Meredith drew from Max embarrassing comparisons with Shakespeare. Today Meredith is remembered largely for two things: his difficult style—it has often been said that he is the only English novelist who needs to be translated into

INTRODUCTION

English—and his presentation of strong, independent women. Meredith was a kind of early feminist. For him the paternalistic, stifling, condescending way in which women were treated was among the basic evils of human existence. His novels feature thinking, spirited women, often clearly superior to their male counterparts. In "Euphemia Clashthought" Max affectionately parodies both Meredith's version of the New Woman and the famous style. Meredith's mannered style can be seen in the opening page of *The Egoist*, where the third paragraph seems almost a self-parody (though it also seems to parody Carlyle):

> Who, says the notable humourist, in allusion to this Book [of Egoism], who can studiously travel through the sheets of leaves now capable of a stretch from the Lizard to the last few poor pulmonary snips and shreds of leagues dancing on their toes for cold, explorers tell us, and catching breath by good luck, like dogs at bones about a table, on the edge of the Pole? Inordinate unvaried length, sheer longinquity, staggers the heart, ages the very heart of us at a view. And how if we manage finally to print one of our pages on the crow-scalp of that solitary majestic outsider? We may with effort get even him into the Book; yet the knowledge we want will not be more present with us than it was when the chapters hung their end over the cliff you ken of at Dover, where sits our great lord and master contemplating the seas without upon the reflex of that within!

"Euphemia Clashthought," only half as obscure, opens with this sentence:

INTRODUCTION

In the heart of insular Cosmos, remote by some scores of leagues of Hodge-trod arable or pastoral, not more than a snuff-pinch for gaping tourist nostrils accustomed to inhalation of prairie winds, but enough for perspective, from those marginal sands, trident-scraped, we are to fancy, by a helmeted Dame Abstract familiarly profiled on discs of current bronze— price of a loaf for humbler maws disdainful of Gallic side-dishes for the titillation of choicer palates— stands Clashthought Park, a house of some pretension, mentioned at Runnymede, with the spreading exception of wings given to it in later times by Daedalean masters not to be baulked of billiards or traps for Terpsichore, and owned for unbroken generations by a healthy line of procreant Clashthoughts, to the undoing of collateral branches eager for the birth of a female.

(The reader of Meredith will catch the "Dame Abstract" echoing Meredith's always capitalized personifications, "Dame Gossip," "Comic Spirit," etc.) Very different from the narrative manner is Meredith's stark, clipped dialogue, deliberately unrealistic, calling attention to itself, much like certain stage dialogue. This Max also captures. Euphemia Clashthought and her fiancé, Sir Rebus, do not accompany the others to Sunday church, because Euphemia dallies and then distracts him with port—(one recalls the famous port scene in *The Egoist*):

"It snows," she murmured, swimming to the window.
"A flake, no more. The season claims it."
"I have thin boots."
"Another pair?"
"My maid buttons. She is at church."

lxx

INTRODUCTION

"My fingers?"

"Ten on each."

"Five," he corrected.

"Buttons."

"I beg your pardon."

The narrator continues:

> She saw opportunity. She swam to the bell-rope and
> grasped it for a tinkle. The action spread feminine
> curves to her lover's eyes. He was a man.
>
> Obsequiousness loomed in the doorways. Its mis-
> tress flashed an order for port—two glasses. Sir
> Rebus sprang a pair of eyebrows on her. Suspicion
> slid down the banisters of his mind, trailing a blue
> ribbon.

(David Garnett recalled the intense delight he experienced when, as a young man reading *The Egoist,* he
picked up Max's parody and read the sentence "Suspicion slid down the banisters of his mind, trailing a blue
ribbon": "Any further comment on Meredith's style,"
Garnett wrote, "was unnecessary.") Euphemia Clashthought, an amalgam of various strong, intelligent, independent women in Meredith, but especially Clara
Middleton of *The Egoist* and Diana Crossways (the
latter name reverberating with "Clashthought"), has
complete control. The port induces sleep in Sir Rebus,
and Euphemia "paddled across the carpet and anon
swam out over the snow. Pagan young womanhood, six
foot of it, spanned eight miles before luncheon." Meredith
was a great propagandist for physical exercise, especially
walking.

G. M. Trevelyan, reflecting perhaps the thought of

many of his generation, said in 1952 that "Euphemia Clashthought" was "still the cleverest parody in all literature."

The original reviewers of *A Christmas Garland* could not agree on which of the parodies were the most successful. But they concurred, with marvelous unanimity, that Max had not merely captured the styles or "externals" of his subjects, but had "unbare[d] their brains and hearts"; he "not only *sounds* like them but actually comes to *look* like them"; he seemed to have obtained "temporary loans of their very minds"; he has "caught the very colour and cast of their minds, and from . . . their attitude to life and letters, he has worked outwards to the perfect jest." Each reader will have a favorite parody, a choice dictated, most likely, by how well he or she knows that author. For Jamesians it will be "The Mote"; for Meredithians it will be "Euphemia Clashthought"; for those who know their Moore it will be "Dickens," and so on.

THIS EDITION

This book reproduces in facsimile the text of the first edition of *A Christmas Garland*, published by William Heinemann in 1912. For this volume Max fussily superintended everything: the binding, including its color, lettering, and the design of the holly wreath; the type, page size, wide margins; and the squarish shape, meant to look, as he said of his own *Zuleika Dobson* (published the previous year), "self-respecting and sober," like a book of essays, and "not like a beastly *novel*." The book contained nine new parodies, one rewritten parody (Meredith) that had been published in the *Saturday Review* in 1896, and seven others (James, Kipling, Wells, Chesterton, Shaw, Hewlett, and Moore) which had first appeared in the same magazine in 1906.

THE CARICATURES

This new edition of *A Christmas Garland* is supplemented with caricatures of the writers parodied. Max maintained that he liked to keep his sister arts apart, but he very often brought them together, as in the illustrations he added to the American edition of *Seven Men*, the color frontispiece he supplied for a late edition of *Zuleika Dobson*, the eighty caricatures he drew for his own copy of *Zuleika Dobson* (published in 1985). Sometimes his two arts were combined when he wrote such lengthy captions to a caricature that the drawing seemed to be illustrating a text. Moreover, Max "improved" various copies of *A Christmas Garland* itself by adding drawings, and from one such copy the eight individual title-page caricatures are reproduced in their places here. He also illustrated a copy of the book for a 1916 Red Cross sale at Christie's (where it fetched 70 guineas), but unfortunately this volume has not been traced. One drawing reproduced here, that of George Moore as a Mexican (Plate 23), was sketched on the final page of the manuscript of the Moore parody.

A further rationale for adding caricatures here arises from the link between caricature and parody. Caricature can be seen as a kind of graphic equivalent of parody. Of course the similarity can be taken only so far—one noteworthy difference is that caricature holds a distorting, highlighting mirror up to nature, while parody holds that mirror up to art. Nonetheless, the connection between caricature and parody is real enough, and what Max wrote about the craft of caricature is also relevant to the craft of parody, about which he wrote very little. He asserted that caricature was "the delicious art of exaggerating, without fear or favour, the peculiarities of this or that human body, for the mere sake of exaggeration"; a good caricature exaggerates all its subject's "salient points," including those of "face, figure, port, gesture and vesture," while diminishing insignificant points. He added that the true caricaturist portrays these salient points simply as they appear to his "distorted gaze." He does not "make conscious aim at exaggeration. He does not say, 'I will go for this "point" or that'.... He exaggerates instinctively, unconsciously." Whether Max deliberately aimed at certain "points" for exaggeration is problematical. But, while concentrating on a man's physical aspects, he manages, consciously or not, to isolate and highlight those salient features that somehow, as he said, get at a person's "soul." He also believed that the caricaturist should never draw from life because he would be "bound by the realities of it." He insisted that caricatures be kept small; they could not, he claimed, abide a large surface. And he preferred economy of line: "In every work of art elimination and simplification are essential. In caricature they are doubly so. For a caricature is a form of wit, and nothing so ruthlessly chokes laughter as the suspicion of labour." Max said that his goal in caricature was "to have the whole thing as absolutely simple as I can.... Just boil a man down to essentials." In the process of producing a successful caricature,

> The whole man must be melted down, as in a crucible, and then, as from the solution, be fashioned anew. He must emerge with not one particle of himself lost, yet with not a particle of himself as it was before. . . . And he will stand there wholly transformed, the joy of his creator, the joy to those who are privy to the art of caricature.

With very little effort one can apply all of this to his parodies: the emphasis on a subject's "salient points" matches the stress on quirks of style; getting indirectly at the "soul" of the man in caricature parallels the parodist's seeming entrance into the very mind of the parodied writer; not drawing from life resembles the practice of not usually parodying a specific single work; the small size of the caricatures corresponds to the brevity of the parodies; economy of line has its counterpart in telling deftness of phrase or sentence; melting the whole man down "as in a crucible" in caricature is comparable to distilling a large work or group of works into one short parody.

To stay for a moment with the notion of "salient points" in caricature: in the drawings reproduced here these points include Henry James's forehead—"more than a dome," Max commented, "it was a whole street"; Kipling's huge jutting jaw, and a curiously diminished back of the head fusing into a thick "brutal" neck atop a small body; Chesterton's enormous girth; Frank Harris's Bismarck mustache, "a tremendous affair"; Bennett's prominent nose, toothy mouth, head thrown back jauntily and confidently; Street's dandyish "vesture"; Gosse's schoolmasterish pose and gesture; Hewlett's "flashing eye"; Moore's wispy, limp hair and the "faintly illumined blank" that was his face. In many of the drawings the caricature looks more like the person than he himself does, even as the parody often sounds more like the writer than the writer himself does.

BIBLIOGRAPHY

MAX BEERBOHM'S PRINCIPAL WRITINGS

The Works of Max Beerbohm. With a bibliography by John Lane. London: The Bodley Head, John Lane, 1896.

The Happy Hypocrite: A Fairy Tale for Tired Men. London and New York: John Lane, The Bodley Head, 1897.

More. London and New York: John Lane, The Bodley Head, 1899.

Zuleika Dobson: Or, An Oxford Love Story. London: William Heinemann, 1911. *The Illustrated Zuleika Dobson,* ed. N. John Hall. New Haven and London: Yale University Press, 1985.

A Christmas Garland: Woven by Max Beerbohm. London: William Heinemann, 1912.

Seven Men. London: William Heinemann, 1919. [Enlarged edition, *Seven Men and Two Others,* Heinemann, 1950.]

And Even Now. London: William Heinemann, 1920.

Around Theatres. 2 vols. London: William Heinemann, 1924.

A Variety of Things. London: William Heinemann, 1928.

The Dreadful Dragon of Hay Hill. London: William Heinemann, 1928.

Lytton Strachey: The Rede Lecture. Cambridge: Cambridge University Press, 1943.

Mainly on the Air. London: William Heinemann, 1946. [Enlarged edition, Heinemann, 1957.]

BIBLIOGRAPHY

More Theatres: 1898–1903. With an introduction by Rupert Hart-Davis. London: Hart-Davis, 1969.

Last Theatres: 1904–1910. With an introduction by Rupert Hart-Davis. London: Hart-Davis, 1970.

A Peep into the Past and Other Prose Pieces by Max Beerbohm. With an introduction by Rupert Hart-Davis. London: William Heinemann, and Brattleboro, Vermont: The Stephen Greene Press, 1972.

Max in Verse: Rhymes and Parodies by Max Beerbohm. Collected and annotated by J. G. Riewald. London: Heinemann, 1969.

BOOKS OF BEERBOHM CARICATURES

Caricatures of Twenty-Five Gentlemen. With an introduction by L. Raven-Hill. London: Leonard Smithers, 1896.

The Poets' Corner. London: William Heinemann, 1904.

A Book of Caricatures. London: Methuen & Co., 1907.

Cartoons: "The Second Childhood of John Bull." London: Stephen Swift, 1911.

Fifty Caricatures. London: William Heinemann, 1913.

A Survey. London: William Heinemann, 1921.

Rossetti and His Circle, London: William Heinemann, 1922. [New edition, with an introduction by N. John Hall. New Haven and London: Yale University Press, 1987].

Things Old and New. London: William Heinemann, 1923.

Observations. London: William Heinemann, 1925.

Heroes and Heroines of Bitter Sweet. London: Messrs Leadlay, Ltd. 1931.

BIBLIOGRAPHY

Caricatures by Max: From the Collection in the Ashmolean Museum. Oxford: Printed for the Ashmolean Museum by Oxford University Press, 1958.

Max's Nineties: Drawings 1892–1899. With an introduction by Osbert Lancaster. London: Rupert Hart-Davis, 1958.

A Catalogue of the Caricatures of Max Beerbohm, compiled by Rupert Hart-Davis. London: Macmillan, 1972.

Beerbohm's Literary Caricatures. With an introduction by J. G. Riewald. London: Allen Lane, 1977.

LETTERS, BIOGRAPHY, AND CRITICISM

Behrman, S. N. *Portrait of Max: An Intimate Memoir of Sir Max Beerbohm*. New York: Random House, 1960; *Conversations with Max*. London: Hamish Hamilton, 1960.

Bross, Addison C. "Beerbohm's 'The Feast' and Conrad's Early Fiction," *Nineteenth-Century Fiction*, 26 (1971), 329–36.

Cecil, David. *Max: A Biography*. London: Constable, 1964.

Danson, Lawrence. *Max Beerbohm and the Act of Writing*. Oxford: Clarendon Press, 1989.

English Literature in Transition: 1880–1920. Max Beerbohm Issue, vol. 27, no. 4 (1984).

Felstiner, John. *The Lies of Art: Max Beerbohm's Parody and Caricature*. New York: Alfred A. Knopf, 1972.

Grushow, Ira. *The Imaginary Reminiscences of Sir Max Beerbohm*. Athens, Ohio: Ohio University Press, 1984.

BIBLIOGRAPHY

Letters of Max Beerbohm: 1892–1956, ed. Rupert Hart-Davis. London: John Murray, 1988.

Lynch, Bohun. *Max in Perspective*. London: Heinemann, 1921.

Max and Will: Max Beerbohm and William Rothenstein: Their Friendship and Letters, ed. Mary M. Lago and Karl Beckson. London: John Murray, 1975.

Max Beerbohm's Letters to Reggie Turner, ed. Rupert Hart-Davis. London: Hart-Davis, 1965.

Riewald, J. G. *Sir Max Beerbohm: Man and Writer*. The Hague: Martinus Nijhoff, 1953.

—— (ed.) *The Surprise of Excellence: Modern Essays on Max Beerbohm*. Hamden, Conn.: Archon Books, 1974.

Viscusi, Robert. *Max Beerbohm, or the Dandy Dante*. Baltimore and London: Johns Hopkins University Press, 1986.

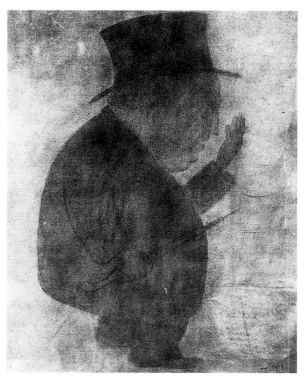

1. London in November and Mr Henry James in London.
   ...It was, therefore, not without something of a
   shock that he, in this to him so very congenial
   atmosphere, now perceived that a vision of the
   hand which he had, at a venture, held up within an
   inch or so of his eyes was, with an almost awful
   clarity being adumbrated...

2. Mr Henry James

3. Mr Rudyard Kipling takes a bloomin' day aht, on the
   blasted 'eath, along with Britannia, 'is gurl

4. Scenes from the Lives of the Poets. Mr Rudyard Kipling composing "The Absent-Minded Beggar"

5. Mr H. G. Wells, prophet and idealist, conjuring up the
   darling Future

6. G. K. Chesterton

7. Mr Thomas Hardy composing a lyric

8. Mr Frank Harris

9. "Had Shakespeare asked me . . ."

10. Mr Arnold Bennett

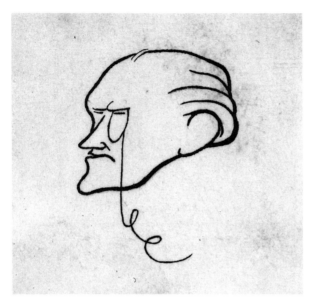

11. John Galsworthy

12. G. S. Street

13. A memory of Henry James and Joseph Conrad conversing at an afternoon party—*circa* 1904

a memory of Henry James and
Joseph Conrad conversing at an afternoon party —
circa 1904.

MB
1926

14. Mr Edmund Gosse

15. Mr Gosse and the Rising Generation. Mr Gosse loquitur: "Diddums!"

16. Henrik Ibsen receiving Mr William Archer in audience

17. Mr Robert Browning taking tea with the Browning Society

18. Mr Hilaire Belloc, striving to win Mr Gilbert Chesterton over from the errors of Geneva

19. The Iconoclast's One Friend.

A Member of Mrs Warren's Profession: "Mr Shaw, I have long wished to meet you, and grasp you by the hand . . . God bless you! . . . I understand that the Army and Navy, the Church, the Stage, the Bar, the Faculty, the Fancy, the Literary Gents, the Nobility and Gentry, and all the Royal Family, will have nothing more to do with you. Never mind. *My* house will always be open to you." (*Exit, dashing away a tear.*)

20. Mr Maurice Hewlett

21. George Moore

22. A Lacuna.

Mr Edmund Gosse (to his interlocutor in "Avowals" [a book by George Moore, largely a dialogue between Moore and Gosse, 1919]): "But, my dear Moore of *course* you will—of *course* they shall! Only, you don't tell us when your seventieth birthday *is*!"

23. George Moore

24. George Meredith. "Our First Novelist"

A CHRISTMAS GARLAND

NOTE

Stevenson, in one of his essays, tells us how he "played the sedulous ape" to Hazlitt, Sir Thomas Browne, Montaigne, and other writers of the past. And the compositors of all our higher-toned newspapers keep the foregoing sentence set up in type always, so constantly does it come tripping off the pens of all higher-toned reviewers. Nor ever do I read it without a fresh thrill of respect for the young Stevenson. I, in my own very inferior boyhood, found it hard to revel in so much as a single page of any writer earlier than Thackeray. This disability I did not shake off, alas, after I left school. There seemed to be so many live authors worth reading. I gave precedence to them, and, not being much of a reader, never had time to grapple with the old masters. Meanwhile, I was already writing a little on my own account. I had had some sort of aptitude for Latin prose and

NOTE

Latin verse. I wondered often whether those two things, essential though they were (and are) to the making of a decent style in English prose, sufficed for the making of a style more than decent. I felt that I must have other models. And thus I acquired the habit of aping, now and again, quite sedulously, this or that live writer—sometimes, it must be admitted, in the hope of learning rather what to avoid. I acquired, too, the habit of publishing these patient little efforts. Some of them appeared in " The Saturday Review " many years ago ; others appeared there more recently. I have selected, by kind permission of the Editor, one from the earlier lot, and seven from the later. The other nine in this book are printed for the first time. The book itself may be taken as a sign that I think my own style is, at length, more or less formed.

M. B.

Rapallo, 1912.

CONTENTS

THE MOTE IN THE MIDDLE DISTANCE

By

H*NRY J*M*S

THE MOTE IN THE MIDDLE DISTANCE

IT was with the sense of a, for him, very memorable something that he peered now into the immediate future, and tried, not without compunction, to take that period up where he had, prospectively, left it. But just where the deuce *had* he left it? The consciousness of dubiety was, for our friend, not, this morning, quite yet clean-cut enough to outline the figures on what she had called his " horizon," between which and himself the twilight was indeed of a quality somewhat intimidating. He had run up, in the course of time, against a good number of " teasers ; " and the function of teasing them back —of, as it were, giving them, every now and then, " what for "—was in him so much a habit that he would have been at a loss had there been, on the face of it, nothing to lose. Oh, he always had offered rewards, of course—had ever so liberally

3

pasted the windows of his soul with staring
appeals, minute descriptions, promises that knew
no bounds. But the actual recovery of the article
—the business of drawing and crossing the
cheque, blotched though this were with tears of
joy—had blankly appeared to him rather in the
light of a sacrilege, casting, he sometimes felt, a
palpable chill on the fervour of the next quest.
It was just this fervour that was threatened as,
raising himself on his elbow, he stared at the foot
of his bed. That his eyes refused to rest there
for more than the fraction of an instant, may be
taken—*was*, even then, taken by Keith Tantalus
—as a hint of his recollection that after all the
phenomenon wasn't to be singular. Thus the
exact repetition, at the foot of Eva's bed, of the
shape pendulous at the foot of *his* was hardly
enough to account for the fixity with which he
envisaged it, and for which he was to find, some
years later, a motive in the (as it turned out)
hardly generous fear that Eva had already made
the great investigation " on her own." Her very
regular breathing presently reassured him that, if
she *had* peeped into " her" stocking, she must
have done so in sleep. Whether he should wake
her now, or wait for their nurse to wake them

both in due course, was a problem presently solved
by a new development. It was plain that his
sister was now watching him between her eyelashes.
He had half expected that. She really was—he
had often told her that she really was—magnificent; and her magnificence was never more
obvious than in the pause that elapsed before she
all of a sudden remarked "They so very indu-
bitably *are*, you know!"

It occurred to him as befitting Eva's remoteness,
which was a part of Eva's magnificence, that her
voice emerged somewhat muffled by the bedclothes.
She was ever, indeed, the most telephonic of her
sex. In talking to Eva you always had, as it
were, your lips to the receiver. If you didn't try
to meet her fine eyes, it was that you simply
couldn't hope to: there were too many dark, too
many buzzing and bewildering and all frankly not
negotiable leagues in between. Snatches of other
voices seemed often to intertrude themselves in
the parley; and your loyal effort not to overhear
these was complicated by your fear of missing
what Eva might be twittering. "Oh, you
certainly haven't, my dear, the trick of pro-
pinquity!" was a thrust she had once parried by
saying that, in that case, *he* hadn't—to which his

unspoken rejoinder that she had caught her tone
from the peevish young women at the Central
seemed to him (if not perhaps in the last, certainly in the last but one, analysis) to lack finality.
With Eva, he had found, it was always safest to
" ring off." It was with a certain sense of his
rashness in the matter, therefore, that he now,
with an air of feverishly " holding the line," said
" Oh, as to that ! "

Had *she*, he presently asked himself, " rung
off " ? It was characteristic of our friend—was
indeed " him all over "—that his fear of what she
was going to say was as nothing to his fear of
what she might be going to leave unsaid. He
had, in his converse with her, been never so
conscious as now of the intervening leagues ; they
had never so insistently beaten the drum of his
ear ; and he caught himself in the act of awfully
computing, with a certain statistical passion, the
distance between Rome and Boston. He has
never been able to decide which of these points he
was psychically the nearer to at the moment when
Eva, replying " Well, one does, anyhow, leave a
margin for the pretext, you know ! " made him,
for the first time in his life, wonder whether she
were not more magnificent than even he had ever

given her credit for being. Perhaps it was to test
this theory, or perhaps merely to gain time, that
he now raised himself to his knees, and, leaning
with outstretched arm towards the foot of his
bed, made as though to touch the stocking which
Santa Claus had, overnight, left dangling there.
His posture, as he stared obliquely at Eva, with
a sort of beaming defiance, recalled to him something seen in an "illustration." This reminis-
cence, however—if such it was, save in the scarred,
the poor dear old woebegone and so very beguil-
ingly *not* refractive mirror of the moment—took
a peculiar twist from Eva's behaviour. She had,
with startling suddenness, sat bolt upright, and
looked to him as if she were overhearing some
tragedy at the other end of the wire, where, in
the nature of things, she was unable to arrest it.
The gaze she fixed on her extravagant kinsman
was of a kind to make him wonder how he con-
trived to remain, as he beautifully did, rigid.
His prop was possibly the reflection that flashed
on him that, if *she* abounded in attenuations, well,
hang it all, so did *he!* It was simply a difference
of plane. Readjust the " values," as painters say,
and there you were! He was to feel that he was
only too crudely " there " when, leaning further

7

forward, he laid a chubby forefinger on the stocking, causing that receptacle to rock ponderously to and fro. This effect was more expected than the tears which started to Eva's eyes, and the intensity with which "Don't you," she exclaimed, "see?"

"The mote in the middle distance?" he asked. "Did you ever, my dear, know me to see anything else? I tell you it blocks out everything. It's a cathedral, it's a herd of elephants, it's the whole habitable globe. Oh, it's, believe me, of an obsessiveness!" But his sense of the one thing it *didn't* block out from his purview enabled him to launch at Eva a speculation as to just how far Santa Claus had, for the particular occasion, gone. The gauge, for both of them, of this seasonable distance seemed almost blatantly suspended in the silhouettes of the two stockings. Over and above the basis of (presumably) sweetmeats in the toes and heels, certain extrusions stood for a very plenary fulfilment of desire. And, since Eva *had* set her heart on a doll of ample proportions and practicable eyelids—*had* asked that most admirable of her sex, their mother, for it with not less directness than he himself had put into his demand for a sword and helmet—her coyness now

8

struck Keith as lying near to, at indeed a hardly measurable distance from, the border-line of his patience. If she didn't *want* the doll, why the deuce had she made such a point of getting it ? He was perhaps on the verge of putting this question to her, when, waving her hand to include both stockings, she said " Of course, my dear, you *do* see. There they are, and you know I know you know we wouldn't, either of us, dip a finger into them." With a vibrancy of tone that seemed to bring her voice quite close to him, " One doesn't," she added, " violate the shrine—pick the pearl from the shell ! "

Even had the answering question " Doesn't one just ? " which for an instant hovered on the tip of his tongue, been uttered, it could not have obscured for Keith the change which her mag- nificence had wrought in him. Something, perhaps, of the bigotry of the convert was already discernible in the way that, averting his eyes, he said " One doesn't even peer." As to whether, in the years that have elapsed since he said this either of our friends (now adult) has, in fact, " peered," is a question which, whenever I call to the house, I am tempted to put to one or

other of them. But any regret I may feel in my
invariable failure to "come up to the scratch" of
yielding to this temptation is balanced, for me,
by my impression—my sometimes all but throned
and anointed certainty — that the answer, if
vouchsafed, would be in the negative.

P.C., X, 36

By

R*D**RD K*PL*NG

P.C., X, 36

Then it's collar 'im tight,
    In the name o' the Lawd !
'Ustle 'im, shake 'im till 'e's sick !
    Wot, 'e *would*, would 'e ? Well,
    Then yer've got ter give 'im 'Ell,
An' it's trunch, trunch, truncheon does the trick !
                    POLICE STATION DITTIES.

I HAD spent Christmas Eve at the Club listening to a grand pow-wow between certain of the choicer sons of Adam. Then Slushby had cut in. Slushby is one who writes to newspapers and is theirs obediently " HUMANITARIAN." When Slushby cuts in, men remember they have to be up early next morning.

Sharp round a corner on the way home, I collided with something firmer than the regulation pillar-box. I righted myself after the recoil and saw some stars that were very pretty indeed. Then I perceived the nature of the obstruction.

" Evening, Judlip," I said sweetly, when I had collected my hat from the gutter. " Have I broken the law, Judlip ? If so, I'll go quiet."

13

"Time yer was in bed," grunted X, 36. "Yer Ma'll be lookin' out for yer."

This from the friend of my bosom! It hurt. Many were the night-beats I had been privileged to walk with Judlip, imbibing curious lore that made glad the civilian heart of me. Seven whole 8 × 5 inch note-books had I pitmanised to the brim with Judlip. And now to be repulsed as one of the uninitiated! It hurt horrid.

There is a thing called Dignity. Small boys sometimes stand on it. Then they have to be kicked. Then they get down, weeping. I don't stand on Dignity.

"What's wrong, Judlip?" I asked, more sweetly than ever. "Drawn a blank to-night?"

"Yuss. Drawn a blank blank blank. 'Avent 'ad so much as a kick at a lorst dorg. Christmas Eve ain't wot it was." I felt for my note-book. "Lawd! I remembers the time when the drunks and disorderlies down this street was as thick as flies on a fly-paper. One just picked 'em orf with one's finger and thumb. A bloomin' battew, that's wot it wos."

"The night's yet young, Judlip," I insinuated, with a jerk of my thumb at the flaring windows of the "Rat and Blood Hound." At that moment the saloon-door swung open, emitting a man and woman who walked with linked arms and exceeding great care.

Judlip eyed them longingly as they tacked up the street. Then he sighed. Now, when Judlip sighs the sound is like unto that which issues from the vent of a Crosby boiler when the cog-gauges are at 260° F.

" Come, Judlip ! " I said. " Possess your soul in patience. You'll soon find someone to make an example of. Meanwhile "—I threw back my head and smacked my lips—" the usual, Judlip ? "

In another minute I emerged through the swing-door, bearing a furtive glass of that same "usual," and nipped down the mews where my friend was wont to await these little tokens of esteem.

" To the Majesty of the Law, Judlip ! "

When he had honoured the toast, I scooted back with the glass, leaving him wiping the beads off his beard-bristles. He was in his philosophic mood when I rejoined him at the corner.

" Wot am I ? " he said, as we paced along. " A bloomin' cypher. Wot's the sarjint ? 'E's got the Inspector over 'im. Over above the Inspector there's the Sooprintendent. Over above 'im's the old red-tape-masticatin' Yard. Over above that there's the 'Ome Sec. Wot's 'e? A cypher, like me. Why?" Judlip looked up at the stars. "Over above 'im's We Dunno Wot. Somethin' wot issues its horders an' regulations an' divisional injunctions, inscrootable like, but p'remptory; an' we 'as ter see as 'ow they're carried out, not arskin' no questions, but each man goin' about 'is dooty.'

"'Is dooty,'" said I, looking up from my note-book. "Yes, I've got that."

"Life ain't a bean-feast. It's a 'arsh reality. An' them as makes it a bean-feast 'as got to be 'arshly dealt with accordin'. That's wot the Force is put 'ere for from Above. Not as 'ow we ain't fallible. We makes our mistakes. An' when we makes 'em we sticks to 'em. For the honour o' the Force. Which same is the jool Britannia wears on 'er bosom as a charm against hanarchy. That's wot the brarsted old Beaks don't understand. Yer remember Smithers of our Div?"

I remembered Smithers—well. As fine, up-standing, square-toed, bullet-headed, clean-living a son of a gun as ever perjured himself in the box. There was nothing of the softy about Smithers. I took off my billicock to Smithers' memory.

16

P.C., X, 36

"Sacrificed to public opinion? Yuss," said Judlip, pausing at a front door and flashing his 45 c.p. down the slot of a two-grade Yale. "Sacrificed to a parcel of screamin' old women wot ort ter 'ave gorn down on their knees an' thanked Gawd for such a protector. 'E'll be out in another 'alf year. Wot'll 'e do then, pore devil? Go a bust on 'is conduc' money an' throw in 'is lot with them same hexperts wot 'ad a 'oly terror of 'im." Then Judlip swore gently.

"What should you do, O Great One, if ever it were your duty to apprehend him?"

"Do? Why, yer blessed innocent, yer don't think I'd shirk a fair clean cop? Same time, I don't say as 'ow I wouldn't 'andle 'im tender like, for sake o' wot 'e wos. Likewise cos 'e'd be a stiff customer to tackle. Likewise 'cos——"

He had broken off, and was peering fixedly upwards at an angle of 85° across the moonlit street. "Ullo!" he said in a hoarse whisper.

Striking an average between the direction of his eyes—for Judlip, when on the job, has a soul-stirring squint—I perceived someone in the act of emerging from a chimney-pot.

17

Judlip's voice clove the silence. "Wot are yer doin' hup there?"

The person addressed came to the edge of the parapet. I saw then that he had a hoary white beard, a red ulster with the hood up, and what looked like a sack over his shoulder. He said something or other in a voice like a concertina that has been left out in the rain.

"I dessay," answered my friend. "Just you come down, an' we'll see about that."

The old man nodded and smiled. Then—as I hope to be saved—he came floating gently down through the moonlight, with the sack over his shoulder and a young fir-tree clasped to his chest. He alighted in a friendly manner on the curb beside us.

Judlip was the first to recover himself. Out went his right arm, and the airman was slung round by the scruff of the neck, spilling his sack in the road. I made a bee-line for his shoulder-blades. Burglar or no burglar, he was the best airman out, and I was muchly desirous to know the precise nature of the apparatus under his ulster. A back-hander from Judlip's left caused me to hop quickly aside. The prisoner was squealing and whimpering. He didn't like

18

the feel of Judlip's knuckles at his cervical vertebræ.

"Wot wos yer doin' hup there?" asked Judlip, tightening the grip.

"I'm S-Santa Claus, Sir. P-please, Sir, let me g-go."

"Hold him," I shouted. "He's a German."

"It's my dooty ter caution yer that wotever yer say now may be used in hevidence against yer, yer old sinner. Pick up that there sack, an' come along o' me."

The captive snivelled something about peace on earth, good will toward men.

"Yuss," said Judlip. "That's in the Noo Testament, ain't it? The Noo Testament contains some uncommon nice readin' for old gents an' young ladies. But it ain't included in the librery o' the Force. We confine ourselves to the Old Testament—O.T., 'ot. An' 'ot you'll get it. Hup with that sack, an' quick march!"

I have seen worse attempts at a neck-wrench, but it was just not slippery enough for Judlip. And the kick that Judlip then let fly was a thing of beauty and a joy for ever.

"Frog's-march him!" I shrieked, dancing. "For the love of heaven, frog's-march him!"

A CHRISTMAS GARLAND

Trotting by Judlip's side to the Station, I reckoned it out that if Slushby had not been at the Club I should not have been here to see. Which shows that even Slushbys are put into this world for a purpose.

OUT OF HARM'S WAY

By

A. C. B*NS*N

OUT OF HARM'S WAY

MORE and more, as the tranquil years went by, Percy found himself able to draw a quiet satisfaction from the regularity, the even sureness, with which, in every year, one season succeeded to another. In boyhood he had felt always a little sad at the approach of autumn. The yellowing leaves of the lime trees, the creeper that flushed to so deep a crimson against the old grey walls, the chrysanthemums that shed so prodigally their petals on the smooth green lawn—all these things, beautiful and wonderful though they were, were somehow a little melancholy also, as being signs of the year's decay. Once, when he was fourteen or fifteen years old, he had overheard a friend of the family say to his father " How the days are drawing in ! "—a remark which set him thinking deeply, with an almost morbid abandonment to gloom, for quite a long time. He had not then grasped the truth that in exactly the proportion in which the days draw in they will, in the fullness

of time, draw out. This was a lesson that he
mastered in later years. And, though the waning
of summer never failed to touch him with the
sense of an almost personal loss, yet it seemed to
him a right thing, a wise ordination, that there
should be these recurring changes. Those men
and women of whom the poet tells us that they
lived in " a land where it was always afternoon "—
could they, Percy often wondered, have felt quite
that thankfulness which on a fine afternoon is felt
by us dwellers in ordinary climes? Ah, no!
Surely it is because we are made acquainted with
the grey sadness of twilight, the solemn majesty
of the night-time, the faint chill of the dawn, that
we set so high a value on the more meridional
hours. If there were no autumn, no winter, then
spring and summer would lose, not all indeed, yet
an appreciable part of their sweet savour for us.
Thus, as his mind matured, Percy came to be very
glad of the gradual changes of the year. He
found in them *a rhythm*, as he once described it in
his diary; and this he liked very much indeed.
He was aware that in his own character, with its
tendency to waywardness, to caprice, to disorder,
there was an almost grievous lack of this *rhythmic*
quality. In the sure and seemly progression of

the months, was there not for him a desirable
exemplar, a needed corrective ? He was so liable
to moods in which he rebelled against the performance of some quite simple duty, some
appointed task—moods in which he said to
himself " H-ng it ! I will not do this," or " Oh,
b-th-r ! I shall not do that ! " But it was clear
that Nature herself never spoke thus. Even as a
passenger in a frail barque on the troublous ocean
will keep his eyes directed towards some upstand-
ing rock on the far horizon, finding thus inwardly
for himself, or hoping to find, a more stable
equilibrium, a deeper tranquillity, than is his,
so did Percy daily devote a certain portion of his
time to quiet communion with the almanac.

There were times when he was sorely tempted
to regret a little that some of the feasts of the
Church were " moveable." True, they moved
only within strictly prescribed limits, and in
accordance with certain unalterable, wholly justifi-
able rules. Yet, in the very fact that they did
move, there seemed—to use an expressive slang
phrase of the day—" something not quite nice."
It was therefore the fixed feasts that pleased
Percy best, and on Christmas Day, especially,
he experienced a temperate glow which would

have perhaps surprised those who knew him only slightly.

By reason of the athletic exercises of his earlier years, Percy had retained in middle life a certain lightness and firmness of tread; and this on Christmas morning, between his rooms and the Cathedral, was always so peculiarly elastic that he might almost have seemed to be rather running than walking. The ancient fane, with its soarings of grey columns to the dimness of its embowed roof, the delicate traceries of the organ screen, the swelling notes of the organ, the mellow shafts of light filtered through the stained-glass windows whose hues were as those of emeralds and rubies and amethysts, the stainless purity of the surplices of clergy and choir, the sober richness of Sunday bonnets in the transept, the faint yet heavy fragrance exhaled from the hot-water pipes—all these familiar things, appealing, as he sometimes felt, almost too strongly to that sensuous side of his nature which made him so susceptible to the paintings of Mr. Leader, of Sir Luke Fildes, were on Christmas morning more than usually affecting by reason of that note of quiet joyousness, of peace and good will, that pervaded the lessons of the day, the collect, the hymns, the sermon.

OUT OF HARM'S WAY

It was this spiritual aspect of Christmas that
Percy felt to be hardly sufficiently regarded, or at
least dwelt on, nowadays, and he sometimes wondered whether the modern Christmas had not
been in some degree inspired and informed by
Charles Dickens. He had for that writer a very
sincere admiration, though he was inclined to
think that his true excellence lay not so much in
faithful portrayal of the life of his times, or in
gift of sustained narration, or in those scenes of
pathos which have moved so many hearts in so
many quiet homes, as in the power of inventing
highly fantastic figures, such as Mr. Micawber or
Mr. Pickwick. This view Percy knew to be
somewhat heretical, and, constitutionally averse
from the danger of being suspected of "talking
for effect," he kept it to himself; but, had anyone
challenged him to give his opinion, it was thus
that he would have expressed himself. In regard
to Christmas, he could not help wishing that
Charles Dickens had laid more stress on its
spiritual element. It was right that the feast
should be an occasion for good cheer, for the
savoury meats, the steaming bowl, the blazing log,
the traditional games. But was not the modern
world, with its almost avowed bias towards

materialism, too little apt to think of Christmas as also a time for meditation, for taking stock, as it were, of the things of the soul? Percy had heard that in London nowadays there was a class of people who sate down to their Christmas dinners in public hotels. He did not condemn this practice. He never condemned a thing, but wondered, rather, whether it were right, and could not help feeling that somehow it was not. In the course of his rare visits to London he had more than once been inside of one of the large new hotels that had sprung up—these " great caravanseries," as he described them in a letter to an old school-fellow who had been engaged for many years in Chinese mission work. And it seemed to him that the true spirit of Christmas could hardly be acclimatised in such places, but found its proper resting-place in quiet, detached homes, where were gathered together only those connected with one another by ties of kinship, or of long and tested friendship.

He sometimes blamed himself for having tended more and more, as the quiet, peaceful, tranquil years went by, to absent himself from even those small domestic gatherings. And yet, might it not be that his instinct for solitude at this season was a

28

right instinct, at least for him, and that to run counter to it would be in some degree unacceptable to the Power that fashioned us? Thus he allowed himself to go, as it were, his own way. After morning service, he sate down to his Christmas fare alone, and then, when the simple meal was over, would sit and think in his accustomed chair, falling perhaps into one of those quiet dozes from which, because they seemed to be so natural a result, so seemly a consummation, of his thoughts, he did not regularly abstain. Later, he sallied forth, with a sense of refreshment, for a brisk walk among the fens, the sedges, the hedge-rows, the reed-fringed pools, the pollard willows that would in due course be putting forth their tender shoots of palest green. And then, once more in his rooms, with the curtains drawn and the candles lit, he would turn to his book-shelves and choose from among them some old book that he knew and loved, or maybe some quite new book by that writer whose works were most dear to him because in them he seemed always to know so precisely what the author would say next, and because he found in their fine-spun repetitions a singular repose, a sense of security, an earnest of calm and continuity, as though he were reading over again one of those wise copy-books that he had so loved in boyhood, or were listening to the sounds made on a piano by some modest, very conscientious young girl with a pale red pig-tail, practising her scales, very gently, hour after hour, next door.

PERKINS AND MANKIND

By

H. G. W★LLS

PERKINS AND MANKIND

Chapter XX

§ 1

IT was the Christmas party at Heighton that was one of the turning-points in Perkins' life. The Duchess had sent him a three-page wire in the hyperbolical style of her class, conveying a vague impression that she and the Duke had arranged to commit suicide together if Perkins didn't " chuck " any previous engagement he had made. And Perkins had felt in a slipshod sort of way—for at this period he was incapable of ordered thought—he might as well be at Heighton as anywhere . . . .

The enormous house was almost full. There must have been upwards of fifty people sitting down to every meal. Many of these were members of the family. Perkins was able to recognise them by their unconvoluted ears—the well-known Grifford ear, transmitted from one generation to another. For the rest there were the usual lot

A CHRISTMAS GARLAND

from the Front Benches and the Embassies. Evesham was there, clutching at the lapels of his coat; and the Prescotts—he with his massive mask of a face, and she with her quick, hawk-like ways, talking about two things at a time; old Tommy Strickland, with his monocle and his dropped g's, telling you what he had once said to Mr. Disraeli; Boubou Seaforth and his American wife; John Pirram, ardent and elegant, spouting old French lyrics; and a score of others.

Perkins had got used to them by now. He no longer wondered what they were " up to," for he knew they were up to nothing whatever. He reflected, while he was dressing for dinner on Christmas night, how odd it was he had ever thought of Using them. He might as well have hoped to Use the Dresden shepherds and shepherdesses that grinned out in the last stages of refinement at him from the glazed cabinets in the drawing-rooms . . . . Or the Labour Members themselves . . . .

True there was Evesham. He had shown an exquisitely open mind about the whole thing. He had at once grasped the underlying principles, thrown out some amazingly luminous suggestions. Oh yes, Evesham was a statesman, right enough.

34

But had even he ever really *believed* in the idea of a Provisional Government of England by the Female Foundlings?

To Perkins the whole thing had seemed so simple, so imminent—a thing that needed only a little general good-will to bring it about. And now . . . Suppose his Bill *had* passed its Second Reading, suppose it had become Law, would this poor old England be by way of functioning decently — after all? Foundlings were sometimes naughty. . . .

What was the matter with the whole human race? He remembered again those words of Scragson's that had had such a depressing effect on him at the Cambridge Union—" Look here, you know! It's all a huge nasty mess, and we're trying to swab it up with a pocket handkerchief." Well, he'd given up trying to do that. . . .

§ 2.

During dinner his eyes wandered furtively up and down the endless ornate table, and he felt he had been, in a sort of way, right in thinking these people were the handiest instrument to prise open the national conscience with. The shining red faces of the men, the shining white necks and arms of the women, the fearless eyes, the general free-and-easiness and spaciousness, the look of late hours counteracted by fresh air and exercise and the best things to eat and drink—what mightn't be made of these people, if they'd only Submit?

Perkins looked behind them, at the solemn young footmen passing and repassing, noiselessly, in blue and white liveries. *They* had Submitted. And it was just because they had been able to that they were no good.

"Damn!" said Perkins, under his breath.

§ 3.

One of the big conifers from the park had been erected in the hall, and this, after dinner, was found to be all lighted up with electric bulbs and hung with packages in tissue paper.

The Duchess stood, a bright, feral figure, distributing these packages to the guests. Perkins' name was called out in due course and the package addressed to him was slipped into his hand. He retired with it into a corner. Inside the tissue-paper was a small morocco leather case. Inside that was a set of diamond and sapphire sleeve-links—large ones.

36

He stood looking at them, blinking a little.

He supposed he must put them on. But something in him, some intractably tough bit of his old self, rose up protesting—frantically.

If he couldn't Use these people, at least they weren't going to Use *him*!

"No, damn it!" he said under his breath, and, thrusting the case into his pocket, slipped away unobserved.

§ 4.

He flung himself into a chair in his bedroom and puffed a blast of air from his lungs. . . . Yes, it had been a narrow escape. He knew that if he had put those beastly blue and white things on he would have been a lost soul. . . .

"You've got to pull yourself together, d'you hear?" he said to himself. "You've got to do a lot of clear, steady, merciless thinking—now, to-night. You've got to persuade yourself somehow that, Foundlings or no Foundlings, this regeneration of mankind business may still be set going—and by *you*."

He paced up and down the room, fuming. How recapture the generous certitudes that had one by one been slipping away from him ? He found himself staring vacantly at the row of books on the little shelf by his bed. One of them seemed suddenly to detach itself — he could almost have sworn afterwards that he didn't reach out for it, but that it hopped down into his hand. . . .

" Sitting Up For The Dawn " ! It was one of that sociological series by which H. G. W∗lls had first touched his soul to finer issues when he was at the 'Varsity.

He opened it with tremulous fingers. Could it re-exert its old sway over him now ?

The page he had opened it at was headed " General Cessation Day," and he began to read. . . .

" The re-casting of the calendar on a decimal basis seems a simple enough matter at first sight. But even here there are details that will have to be thrashed out. . . .

" Mr. Edgar Dibbs, in his able pamphlet ' Ten to the Rescue,' [1] advocates a twenty-hour day, and has drawn up an ingenious scheme for accelerating the motion of this planet by four in every twenty-

[1] Published by the Young Self-Helpers' Press, Ipswich.

four hours, so that the alternations of light and
darkness shall be re-adjusted to the new reckoning.
I think such re-adjustment would be indispensable
(though I know there is a formidable body of
opinion against me).   But I am far from being
convinced of the feasibility of Mr. Dibbs' scheme.
I believe the twenty-four hour day has come to
stay—anomalous though it certainly will seem in
the ten-day week, the fifty-day month, and the
thousand-day year.   I should like to have incor-
porated Mr. Dibbs' scheme in my vision of the
Dawn.   But, as I have said, the scope of this
vision is purely practical. . . .

"Mr. Albert Baker, in a paper [1] read before the
South Brixton Hebdomadals, pleads that the first
seven days of the decimal week should retain their
old names, the other three to be called provision-
ally Huxleyday, Marxday, and Tolstoiday.   But,
for reasons which I have set forth elsewhere,[2] I
believe that the   nomenclature which I had
originally suggested [3]—Aday, Bday, and so on to
Jday—would be really the simplest way out of
the difficulty.   Any fanciful way of naming the

[1] "Are We Going Too Fast?"
[2] "A Midwife For The Millennium."   H. G. W*lls.
[3] "How To Be Happy Though Yet Unborn."   H. G. W*lls.

days would be bad, as too sharply differentiating one day from another. What we must strive for in the Dawn is that every day shall be as nearly as possible like every other day. We must help the human units—these little pink slobbering creatures of the Future whose cradle we are rocking—to progress not in harsh jerks, but with a beautiful unconscious rhythm. . . .

"There must be nothing corresponding to our Sunday. Sunday is a canker that must be cut ruthlessly out of the social organism. At present the whole community gets 'slack' on Saturday because of the paralysis that is about to fall on it. And then 'Black Monday'!—that day when the human brain tries to readjust itself—tries to realise that the shutters are down, and the streets are swept, and the stove-pipe hats are back in their band-boxes. . . .

"Yet of course there must be holidays. We can no more do without holidays than without sleep. For every man there must be certain stated intervals of repose—of recreation in the original sense of the word. My views on the worthlessness of classical education are perhaps pretty well known to you, but I don't underrate the great service that my friend Professor Ezra K.

PERKINS AND MANKIND

Higgins has rendered by his discovery [1] that the word recreation originally signified a re-creating— i.e.,[2] a time for the nerve-tissues to renew themselves in. The problem before us is how to secure for the human units in the Dawn—these giants of whom we are but the fœtuses—the holidays necessary for their full capacity for usefulness to the State, without at the same time disorganising the whole community—and them.

" The solution is really very simple. The community will be divided into ten sections—Section A, Section B, and so on to Section J. And to every section one day of the decimal week will be assigned as a ' Cessation Day.' Thus, those people who fall under Section A will rest on Aday, those who fall under Section B will rest on Bday, and so on. On every day of the year one-tenth of the population will be resting, but the other nine-tenths will be at work. The joyous hum and clang of labour will never cease in the municipal workshops. . . .

" You figure the smokeless blue sky above London dotted all over with airships in which the

[1] "Words About Words." By Ezra K. Higgins, Professor of Etymology, Abraham Z. Stubbins University, Padua, Pa., U.S.A. (2 vols.).
[2] " *Id est* "—",That is."

41

holiday-making tenth are re-creating themselves for the labour of next week—looking down a little wistfully, perhaps, at the workshops from which they are temporarily banished. And here I scent a difficulty. So attractive a thing will labour be in the Dawn that a man will be tempted not to knock off work when his Cessation Day comes round, and will prefer to work for no wage rather than not at all. So that perhaps there will have to be a law making Cessation Day compulsory, and the Overseers will be empowered to punish infringement of this law by forbidding the culprit to work for ten days after the first offence, twenty after the second, and so on. But I don't suppose there will often be need to put this law in motion. The children of the Dawn, remember, will not be the puny self-ridden creatures that we are. They will not say, ' Is this what I want to do ? ' but ' Shall I, by doing this, be (a) harming or (b) benefiting—no matter in how infinitesimal a degree—the Future of the Race ? '

"Sunday must go. And, as I have hinted, the progress of mankind will be steady proportionately to its own automatism. Yet I think there would be no harm in having one—just one—day in the year set aside as a day of universal rest—

a day for the searching of hearts. Heaven—I
mean the Future—forbid that I should be hide-
bound by dry-as-dust logic, in dealing with
problems of flesh and blood. The sociologists of
the past thought the grey matter of their own
brains all-sufficing. They forgot that flesh is
pink and blood is red. That is why they could
not convert people. . . .

"The five-hundredth and last day of each year
shall be a General Cessation Day. It will correspond somewhat to our present Christmas Day.
But with what a difference! It will not be, as
with us, a mere opportunity for relatives to make
up the quarrels they have picked with each other
during the past year, and to eat and drink things
that will make them ill well into next year.
Holly and mistletoe there will be in the Municipal
Eating Rooms, but the men and women who sit
down there to General Cessation High-Tea will
be glowing not with a facile affection for their
kith and kin, but with communal anxiety for the
welfare of the great-great-grand-children of
people they have never met and are never likely
to meet.

"The great event of the day will be the performance of the ceremony of 'Making Way.'

" In the Dawn, death will not be the haphazard affair that it is under the present anarchic conditions. Men will not be stumbling out of the world at odd moments and for reasons over which they have no control. There will always, of course, be a percentage of deaths by misadventure. But there will be no deaths by disease. Nor, on the other hand, will people die of old age. Every child will start life knowing that (barring misadventure) he has a certain fixed period of life before him—so much and no more, but not a moment less.

" It is impossible to foretell to what average age the children of the Dawn will retain the use of all their faculties—be fully vigorous mentally and physically. We only know they will be ' going strong ' at ages when we have long ceased to be any use to the State. Let us, for sake of argument, say that on the average their faculties will have begun to decay at the age of ninety— a trifle over thirty-two, by the new reckoning. That, then, will be the period of life fixed for all citizens. Every man on fulfilling that period will avail himself of the Municipal Lethal Chamber. He will ' make way '. . . .

"I thought at one time that it would be best

PERKINS AND MANKIND

for every man to 'make way' on the actual day
when he reaches the age-limit. But I see now
that this would savour of private enterprise.
Moreover, it would rule out that element of
sentiment which, in relation to such a thing as
death, we must do nothing to mar. The children
and friends of a man on the brink of death would
instinctively wish to gather round him. How
could they accompany him to the lethal chamber,
if it were an ordinary working-day, with every
moment of the time mapped out for them ?

"On General Cessation Day, therefore, the
gates of the lethal chambers will stand open for
all those who shall in the course of the past year
have reached the age-limit. You figure the wide
streets filled all day long with little solemn
processions—solemn and yet not in the least
unhappy. . . . You figure the old man walking
with a firm step in the midst of his progeny,
looking around him with a clear eye at this dear
world which is about to lose him. He will not
be thinking of himself. He will not be wishing
the way to the lethal chamber was longer. He
will be filled with joy at the thought that he is
about to die for the good of the race—to 'make
way' for the beautiful young breed of men and

45

women who, in simple, artistic, antiseptic garments, are disporting themselves so gladly on this day of days. They pause to salute him as he passes. And presently he sees, radiant in the sunlight, the pleasant white-tiled dome of the lethal chamber. You figure him at the gate, shaking hands all round, and speaking perhaps a few well-chosen words about the Future. . . ."

§ 5

It was enough. The old broom hadn't lost its snap. It had swept clean the chambers of Perkins' soul—swished away the whole accumulation of nasty little cobwebs and malignant germs. Gone were the mean doubts that had formed in him, the lethargy, the cheap cynicism. Perkins was himself again.

He saw now how very stupid it was of him to have despaired just because his own particular panacea wasn't given a chance. That Provisional Government plan of his had been good, but it was only one of an infinite number of possible paths to the Dawn. He would try others—scores of others . . . .

He must get right away out of here—to-night.

46

PERKINS AND MANKIND

He must have his car brought round from the garage—now—to a side door . . . .

But first he sat down to the writing-table, and wrote quickly:

Dear Duchess,

I regret I am called away on urgent political business . . . .

Yours faithfully
J. Perkins . . . .

He took the morocco leather case out of his pocket and enclosed it, with the note, in a large envelope.

Then he pressed the electric button by his bedside, almost feeling that this was a signal for the Dawn to rise without more ado . . . .

SOME DAMNABLE
ERRORS ABOUT
CHRISTMAS
By
G. K. CH★ST★RT★N

SOME DAMNABLE ERRORS
ABOUT CHRISTMAS

THAT it is human to err is admitted by even
the most positive of our thinkers. Here we
have the great difference between latter-day
thought and the thought of the past. If Euclid
were alive to-day (and I dare say he is) he would
not say, "The angles at the base of an isosceles
triangle are equal to one another." He would
say, "To me (a very frail and fallible being,
remember) it does somehow seem that these two
angles have a mysterious and awful equality to
one another." The dislike of schoolboys for
Euclid is unreasonable in many ways ; but
fundamentally it is entirely reasonable. Fundamentally it is the revolt from a man who was
either fallible and therefore (in pretending to
infallibility) an impostor, or infallible and therefore not human.

Now, since it is human to err, it is always in
reference to those things which arouse in us the
most human of all our emotions—I mean the
emotion of love—that we conceive the deepest of

our errors. Suppose we met Euclid on Westminster Bridge, and he took us aside and confessed
to us that whilst he regarded parallelograms and
rhomboids with an indifference bordering on
contempt, for isosceles triangles he cherished a
wild romantic devotion. Suppose he asked us to
accompany him to the nearest music-shop, and
there purchased a guitar in order that he might
worthily sing to us the radiant beauty and the
radiant goodness of isosceles triangles. As men
we should, I hope, respect his enthusiasm, and
encourage his enthusiasm, and catch his enthusiasm. But as seekers after truth we should be
compelled to regard with a dark suspicion, and to
check with the most anxious care, every fact that
he told us about isosceles triangles. For adora-
tion involves a glorious obliquity of vision. It
involves more than that. We do not say of Love
that he is short-sighted. We do not say of Love
that he is myopic. We do not say of Love that
he is astigmatic. We say quite simply, Love is
blind. We might go further and say, Love is
deaf. That would be a profound and obvious
truth. We might go further still and say, Love
is dumb. But that would be a profound and
obvious lie. For love is always an extraordinarily

ERRORS ABOUT CHRISTMAS

fluent talker. Love is a wind-bag, filled with a gusty wind from Heaven.

It is always about the thing that we love most that we talk most. About this thing, therefore, our errors are something more than our deepest errors: they are our most frequent errors. That is why for nearly two thousand years mankind has been more glaringly wrong on the subject of Christmas than on any other subject. If mankind had hated Christmas, he would have understood it from the first. What would have happened then, it is impossible to say. For that which is hated, and therefore is persecuted, and therefore grows brave, lives on for ever, whilst that which is understood dies in the moment of our understanding of it—dies, as it were, in our awful grasp. Between the horns of this eternal dilemma shivers all the mystery of the jolly visible world, and of that still jollier world which is invisible. And it is because Mr. Shaw and the writers of his school cannot, with all their splendid sincerity and acumen, perceive that he and they and all of us are impaled on those horns as certainly as the sausages I ate for breakfast this morning had been impaled on the cook's toasting-fork—it is for this reason, I say, that Mr. Shaw and his friends seem to me to miss the basic principle that lies at the root of all things human and divine. By the way, not all things that are divine are human. But all things that are human are divine. But to return to Christmas.

I select at random two of the more obvious fallacies that obtain. One is that Christmas should be observed as a time of jubilation. This is (I admit) quite a recent idea. It never entered into the tousled heads of the shepherds by night, when the light of the angel of the Lord shone about them and they arose and went to do homage to the Child. It never entered into the heads of the Three Wise Men. They did not bring their gifts as a joke, but as an awful oblation. It never entered into the heads of the saints and scholars, the poets and painters, of the Middle Ages. Looking back across the years, they saw in that dark and ungarnished manger only a shrinking woman, a brooding man, and a child born to sorrow. The philomaths of the eighteenth century, looking back, saw nothing at all. It is not the least of the glories of the Victorian Era that it rediscovered Christmas. It is not the least of the mistakes of the Victorian Era that it supposed Christmas to be a feast.

ERRORS ABOUT CHRISTMAS

The splendour of the saying, "I have piped unto you, and you have not danced; I have wept with you, and you have not mourned" lies in the fact that it might have been uttered with equal truth by any man who had ever piped or wept. There is in the human race some dark spirit of recalcitrance, always pulling us in the direction contrary to that in which we are reasonably expected to go. At a funeral, the slightest thing, not in the least ridiculous at any other time, will convulse us with internal laughter. At a wedding, we hover mysteriously on the brink of tears. So it is with the modern Christmas. I find myself in agreement with the cynics in so far that I admit that Christmas, as now observed, tends to create melancholy. But the reason for this lies solely in our own misconception. Christmas is essentially a *dies iræ*. If the cynics will only make up their minds to treat it as such, even the saddest and most atrabilious of them will acknowledge that he has had a rollicking day.

This brings me to the second fallacy. I refer to the belief that "Christmas comes but once a year." Perhaps it does, according to the calendar —a quaint and interesting compilation, but of little or no practical value to anybody. It is not the calendar, but the Spirit of Man that regulates the recurrence of feasts and fasts. Spiritually, Christmas Day recurs exactly seven times a week. When we have frankly acknowledged this, and acted on this, we shall begin to realise the Day's mystical and terrific beauty. For it is only every-day things that reveal themselves to us in all their wonder and their splendour. A man who happens one day to be knocked down by a motor-bus merely utters a curse and instructs his solicitor, but a man who has been knocked down by a motor-bus every day of the year will have begun to feel that he is taking part in an august and soul-cleansing ritual. He will await the diurnal stroke of fate with the same lowly and pious joy as animated the Hindoos awaiting Juggernaut. His bruises will be decorations, worn with the modest pride of the veteran. He will cry aloud, in the words of the late W. E. Henley, "My head is bloody but unbowed." He will add, "My ribs are broken but unbent."

I look for the time when we shall wish one another a Merry Christmas every morning; when roast turkey and plum-pudding shall be the staple of our daily dinner, and the holly shall never be taken down from the walls, and everyone will

always be kissing everyone else under the mistletoe.
And what is right as regards Christmas is right
as regards all other so-called anniversaries. The
time will come when we shall dance round the
Maypole every morning before breakfast—a meal
at which hot-cross buns will be a standing dish—
and shall make April fools of one another every
day before noon. The profound significance of
All Fool's Day—the glorious lesson that we are
all fools—is too apt at present to be lost. Nor is
justice done to the sublime symbolism of Shrove
Tuesday—the day on which all sins are shriven.
Every day pancakes shall be eaten, either before
or after the plum-pudding. They shall be eaten
slowly and sacramentally. They shall be fried
over fires tended and kept for ever bright by
Vestals. They shall be tossed to the stars.

I shall return to the subject of Christmas next
week.

A SEQUELULA TO
"THE DYNASTS"

By

TH*M*S H*RDY

A SEQUELULA TO "THE DYNASTS" [1]

The Void is disclosed.   Our own Solar System is visible,
distant by some two million miles.
Enter the Ancient Spirit and Chorus of the Years, the
Spirit and Chorus of the Pities, the Spirit Ironic,
the Spirit Sinister, Rumours, Spirit-Messengers,
and the Recording Angel.

SPIRIT OF THE PITIES.

Yonder, that swarm of things insectual
Wheeling Nowhither in Particular—
What is it?

SPIRIT OF THE YEARS.

That ? Oh that is merely one
Of those innumerous congeries
Of parasites by which, since time began,
Space has been interfested.

SPIRIT SINISTER.

What a pity
We have no means of stamping out these pests !

[1] *This has been composed from a scenario thrust on me by
some one else.   My philosophy of life saves me from sense of
responsibility for any of my writings ; but I venture to hold
myself specially irresponsible for this one.*—TH*M*S H*RDY.

A CHRISTMAS GARLAND

Nay, but I like to watch them buzzing round,
Poor little trumpery ephaeonals!

CHORUS OF THE PITIES (aerial music).

Yes, yes!
What matter a few more or less?
Here and Nowhere plus
Whence and Why makes Thus.
Let these things be.
There's room in the world for them and us.

Nothing is,
Out in the vast immensities
Where these things flit,
Irrequisite
In a minor key
To the tune of the sempiternal It.

SPIRIT IRONIC.

The curious thing about them is that some
Have lesser parasites adherent to them—
Bipedular and quadrupedular
Infinitesimals.   On close survey
You see these movesome.   Do you not recall,

62

SEQUELULA TO 'THE DYNASTS'

We once went in a party and beheld
All manner of absurd things happening
On one of those same—planets, don't you call them?

S<small>PIRIT</small> OF THE Y<small>EARS</small> (screwing up his eyes at the
Solar System).

One of that very swarm it was, if I mistake not.
It had a parasite that called itself
Napoléon.   And lately, I believe,
Another parasite has had the impudence
To publish an elaborate account
Of our (for so we deemed it) private visit.

S<small>PIRIT</small> S<small>INISTER</small>.

His name?

R<small>ECORDING</small> A<small>NGEL</small>.
One moment.

(Turns over leaves.)

Hardy, Mr. Thomas,
Novelist.   Author of " The Woodlanders,"
" Far from the Madding Crowd," " The Trum-
pet Major,"
" Tess of the D'Urbervilles," etcetera,
Etcetera.   In 1895
" Jude the Obscure " was published, and a few

A CHRISTMAS GARLAND

Hasty reviewers, having to supply
A column for the day of publication,
Filled out their space by saying that there were
Several passages that might have been
Omitted with advantage.   Mr. Hardy
Saw that if that was so, well then, of course,
Obviously the only thing to do
Was to write no more novels, and forthwith
Applied himself to drama, and to Us.

SPIRIT IRONIC.

Let us hear what he said about Us.

THE OTHER SPIRITS.

Let's.

RECORDING ANGEL. (raising receiver of aerial
telephone).

3 oh 4 oh oh 3 5, Space. . . . Hulloa.
Is that the Superstellar Library ?
I'm the Recording Angel.   Kindly send me
By Spirit-Messenger a copy of
" The Dynasts " by T. Hardy.   Thank you.

A pause.   Enter Spirit-Messenger, with copy
of " The Dynasts."

Thanks.

64

SEQUELULA TO 'THE DYNASTS'

Exit Spirit-Messenger. The Recording Angel reads "The Dynasts" aloud.

Just as the reading draws to a close, enter the Spirit of Mr. Clement Shorter and Chorus of Subtershorters. They are visible as small grey transparencies swiftly interpenetrating the brains of the spatial Spirits.

SPIRIT OF THE PITIES.

It is a book which, once you take it up,
You cannot readily lay down.

SPIRIT SINISTER.

There is

Not a dull page in it.

SPIRIT OF THE YEARS.

A bold conception
Outcarried with that artistry for which
The author's name is guarantee.   We have
No hesitation in commending to our readers
A volume which—

The Spirit of Mr. Clement Shorter and Chorus of Subtershorters are detected and expelled.

—we hasten to denounce
As giving an entirely false account
Of our impressions.

A CHRISTMAS GARLAND

Spirit Ironic.

Hear, *hear !*

Spirit Sinister.

Hear, *hear !*

Spirit of the Pities.

Hear !

Spirit of the Years.

Intensive vision has this Mr. Hardy,
With a dark skill in weaving word-patterns
Of subtle ideographies that mark him
A man of genius.   So am not I,
But a plain Spirit, simple and forthright,
With no damned philosophical fal-lals
About me.   When I visited that planet
And watched the animalculae thereon,
I never said they were " automata "
And "jackaclocks," nor dared describe their deeds
As " Life's impulsion by Incognizance."
It may be that those mites have no free will,
But how should I know ? Nay, how Mr. Hardy ?
We cannot glimpse the origin of things,
Cannot conceive a Causeless Cause, albeit

66

SEQUELULA TO 'THE DYNASTS'

Such a Cause must have been, and must be greater
Than we whose little wits cannot conceive it.
" Incognizance " ! Why deem incognizant
An infinitely higher than ourselves ?
How dare define its way with us ?   How know
Whether it leaves us free or holds us bond ?

SPIRIT OF THE PITIES.

Allow me to associate myself
With every word that's fallen from your lips.
The author of " The Dynasts " has indeed
Misused his undeniably great gifts
In striving to belittle things that are
Little enough already.   I don't say
That the phrenetical behaviour
Of those aforesaid animalculae
Did, while we watched them, seem to indicate
Possession of free-will.   But, bear in mind,
We saw them in peculiar circumstances—
At war, blinded with blood and lust and fear.
Is it not likely that at other times
They are quite decent midgets, capable
Of thinking for themselves, and also acting
Discreetly on their own initiative,
Not drilled and herded, yet gregarious—
A wise yet frolicsome community ?

67

A CHRISTMAS GARLAND

Spirit Ironic.

What are *these "other times" though? I had*
    thought
Those midgets whiled away the vacuous hours
After one war in training for the next.
And let me add that my contempt for them
Is not done justice to by Mr. Hardy.

Spirit Sinister.

Nor mine.   And I have reason to believe
Those midgets shone above their average
When we inspected them.

A Rumour (tactfully intervening).

              Yet have I heard
(Though not on very good authority)
That once a year they hold a festival
And thereat all with one accord unite
In brotherly affection and good will.

Spirit of the Years (to Recording Angel).

Can you authenticate this Rumour?

Recording Angel.

Such festival they have, and call it " Christmas."

SEQUELULA TO 'THE DYNASTS'

SPIRIT OF THE PITIES.

Then let us go and reconsider them
Next " Christmas."

SPIRIT OF THE YEARS (to Recording Angel).

When is that ?

RECORDING ANGEL (consults terrene calendar).

This day three weeks.

SPIRIT OF THE YEARS.

On that day we will re-traject ourselves.
Meanwhile, 'twere well we should be posted up
In details of this feast.

SPIRIT OF THE PITIES (to Recording Angel).

Aye, tell us more.

RECORDING ANGEL.

I fancy you could best find what you need
In the Complete Works of the late Charles
Dickens.
I have them here.

SPIRIT OF THE YEARS.

Read them aloud to us.

69

A CHRISTMAS GARLAND

The Recording Angel reads aloud the Complete Works
of Charles Dickens.

RECORDING ANGEL (closing " Edwin Drood ").

'Tis Christmas Morning.

SPIRIT OF THE YEARS.

Then must we away.

SEMICHORUS I. OF YEARS (aerial music).

'Tis time we press on to revisit
  That dear little planet,
To-day of all days to be seen at
  Its brightest and best.

Now holly and mistletoe girdle
  Its halls and its homesteads,
And every biped is beaming
  With peace and good will.

SEMICHORUS II.

With good will and why not with free will ?
  If clearly the former
May nest in those bosoms, then why not
  The latter as well ?

70

SEQUELULA TO 'THE DYNASTS'

Let's lay down no laws to trip up on,
 Our way is in darkness,
And not but by groping unhampered
 We win to the light.

The Spirit and Chorus of the Years traject themselves,
closely followed by the Spirit and Chorus of the
Pities, the Spirits and Choruses Sinister and Ironic,
Rumours, Spirit Messengers, and the Recording
Angel.

There is the sound of a rushing wind. The Solar
System is seen for a few instants growing larger
and larger—a whorl of dark, vastening orbs career-
ing round the sun. All but one of these is
lost to sight. The convex seas and continents of
our planet spring into prominence.

The Spirit of Mr. Hardy is visible as a grey trans-
parency swiftly interpenetrating the brain of the
Spirit of the Years, and urging him in a particular
direction, to a particular point.

The Aerial Visitants now hover in mid-air on the outskirts of Casterbridge, Wessex, immediately above
the County Gaol.

SPIRIT OF THE YEARS.

First let us watch the revelries within
This well-kept castle whose great walls connote
A home of the pre-eminently blest.

The roof of the gaol becomes transparent, and the whole
interior is revealed, like that of a beehive under
glass.

71

A CHRISTMAS GARLAND

Warders are marching mechanically round the corridors
of white stone, unlocking and clanging open the
iron doors of the cells. Out from every door steps
a convict, who stands at attention, his face to the
wall.

At a word of command the convicts fall into gangs
of twelve, and march down the stone stairs, out
into the yard, where they line up against the walls.

Another word of command, and they file mechanically,
but not more mechanically than their warders, into
the Chapel.

SPIRIT OF THE PITIES.

Enough!

SPIRITS SINISTER AND IRONIC.

'Tis more than even we can bear.

SPIRIT OF THE PITIES.

Would we had never come!

SPIRIT OF THE YEARS.

Brother, 'tis well
To have faced a truth however hideous,
However humbling. Gladly I discipline
My pride by taking back those pettish doubts
Cast on the soundness of the central thought
In Mr. Hardy's drama. He was right.

72

SEQUELULA TO 'THE DYNASTS'

Automata these animalculae
Are—puppets, pitiable jackaclocks.
Be't as it may elsewhere, upon this planet
There's no free will, only obedience
To some blind, deaf, unthinking despotry
That justifies the horridest pessimism.
Frankly acknowledging all this, I beat
A quick but not disorderly retreat.

> He re-trajects himself into Space, followed closely by
> his Chorus, and by the Spirit and Chorus of the
> Pities, the Spirits Sinister and Ironic with their
> Choruses, Rumours, Spirit Messengers, and the
> Recording Angel.

SHAKESPEARE AND CHRISTMAS

By

FR*NK H*RR*S

SHAKESPEARE AND
CHRISTMAS

THAT Shakespeare hated Christmas—hated
it with a venom utterly alien to the gentle
heart in him—I take to be a proposition that
establishes itself automatically. If there is one
thing lucid-obvious in the Plays and Sonnets, it
is Shakespeare's unconquerable loathing of Christmas. The Professors deny it, however, or deny
that it is proven. With these gentlemen I will
deal faithfully. I will meet them on their own
parched ground, making them fertilise it by
shedding there the last drop of the water that
flows through their veins.

If you find, in the works of a poet whose
instinct is to write about everything under the
sun, one obvious theme untouched, or touched
hardly at all, then it is at least presumable that
there was some good reason for that abstinence.
Such a poet was Shakespeare. It was one of the
divine frailties of his genius that he must be ever
flying off at a tangent from his main theme to
unpack his heart in words about some frivolous-

small irrelevance that had come into his head. If it could be shown that he never mentioned Christmas, we should have proof presumptive that he consciously avoided doing so. But if the fact is that he did mention it now and again, but in grudging fashion, without one spark of illumination—he, the arch-illuminator of all things—then we ·have proof positive that he detested it.

I see Dryasdust thumbing his Concordance. Let my memory save him the trouble. I will reel him off the one passage in which Shakespeare spoke of Christmas in words that rise to the level of mediocrity.

> Some say that ever 'gainst that season comes
> Wherein our Saviour's birth is celebrated,
> The bird of dawning singeth all night long :
> And then, they say, no spirit dare stir abroad ;
> The nights are wholesome ; then no planets strike,
> No fairy takes, nor witch hath power to charm,
> So hallowed and so gracious is the time.

So says Marcellus at Elsinore. This is the best our Shakespeare can vamp up for the birthday of the Man with whom he of all men had the most in common. And Dryasdust, eternally unable to distinguish chalk from cheese, throws up his hands in admiration of the marvellous poetry. If

SHAKESPEARE AND CHRISTMAS

Dryasdust had written it, it would more than pass muster. But as coming from Shakespeare, how feeble-cold—aye, and sulky-sinister! The greatest praiser the world will ever know!—and all he can find in his heart to sing of Christmas is a stringing-together of old women's superstitions! Again and again he has painted Winter for us as it never has been painted since—never by Goethe even, though Goethe in more than one of the *Winter-Lieder* touched the hem of his garment. There was every external reason why he should sing, as only he could have sung, of Christmas. The Queen set great store by it. She and her courtiers celebrated it year by year with lusty-pious unction. And thus the ineradicable snob in Shakespeare had the most potent of all inducements to honour the feast with the full power that was in him. But he did not, because he would not. What is the key to the enigma?

For many years I hunted it vainly. The second time that I met Carlyle I tried to enlist his sympathy and aid. He sat pensive for a while and then said that it seemed to him " a goose-quest." I replied, " You have always a phrase for everything, Tom, but always the wrong one." He covered his face, and presently, peering at me through his gnarled fingers, said " Mon, ye're recht." I discussed the problem with Renan, with Emerson, with Disraeli, also with Cetewayo—poor Cetewayo, best and bravest of men, but intellectually a Professor, like the rest of them. It was borne in on me that if I were to win to the heart of the mystery I must win alone.

The solution, when suddenly it dawned on me, was so simple-stark that I was ashamed of the ingenious-clever ways I had been following. (I learned then—and perhaps it is the one lesson worth the learning of any man—that truth may be approached only through the logic of the heart. For the heart is eye and ear, and all excellent understanding abides there.) On Christmas Day, assuredly, Anne Hathaway was born.

In what year she was born I do not know nor care. I take it she was not less than thirty-eight when she married Shakespeare. This, however, is sheer conjecture, and in no way important-apt to our inquiry. It is not the year, but the day of the year, that matters. All we need bear in mind is that on Christmas Day that woman was born into the world.

If there be any doubting Thomas among my

SHAKESPEARE AND CHRISTMAS

readers, let him not be afraid to utter himself.
I am (with the possible exception of Shakespeare)
the gentlest man that ever breathed, and I do but
bid him study the Plays in the light I have given
him. The first thing that will strike him is that
Shakespeare's thoughts turned constantly to the
birthdays of all his Fitton-heroines, as a lover's
thoughts always do turn to the moment at which
the loved one first saw the light. "There was a
star danced, and under that" was born Beatrice.
Juliet was born "on Lammas Eve." Marina
tells us she derived her name from the chance of
her having been "born at sea." And so on,
througnout the whole gamut of women in whom
Mary Fitton was bodied forth to us. But mark
how carefully Shakespeare says never a word about
the birthdays of the various shrews and sluts in
whom, again and again, he gave us his wife.
When and were was born Queen Constance, the
scold? And Bianca? And Doll Tearsheet, and
"Greasy Jane" in the song, and all the rest of
them? It is of the last importance that we
should know. Yet never a hint is vouchsafed us
in the text. It is clear that Shakespeare cannot
bring himself to write about Anne Hathaway's
birthday—will not stain his imagination by think-

ing of it.   That is entirely human-natural.   But
why should he loathe Christmas Day itself with
precisely the same loathing?   There is but one
answer—and that inevitable-final.   The two days
were one.

Some soul-secrets are so terrible that the most
hardened realist of us may well shrink from laying
them bare.   Such a soul-secret was this of Shakespeare's.   Think of it!   The gentlest spirit that
ever breathed, raging and fuming endlessly in
impotent-bitter spleen against the prettiest of
festivals!   Here is a spectacle so tragic-piteous
that, try as we will, we shall not put it from us.
And it is well that we should not, for in our
plenary compassion we shall but learn to love the
man the more.

[*Mr. Fr*nk H*rr*s is very much a man of genius, and **I**
should be sorry if this adumbration of his manner made any
one suppose that I do not rate his writings about Shakespeare
higher than those of all " the Professors" together.*—M. B.]

SCRUTS

By

ARN*LD B*NN*TT

SCRUTS

I

EMILY WRACKGARTH stirred the Christmas pudding till her right arm began to ache. But she did not cease for that. She stirred on till her right arm grew so numb that it might have been the right arm of some girl at the other end of Bursley. And yet something deep down in her whispered " It is *your* right arm! And you can do what you like with it ! "

She did what she liked with it. Relentlessly she kept it moving till it reasserted itself as the arm of Emily Wrackgarth, prickling and tingling as with red-hot needles in every tendon from wrist to elbow. And still Emily Wrackgarth hardened her heart.

Presently she saw the spoon no longer revolving, but wavering aimlessly in the midst of the basin. Ridiculous! This must be seen to! In the down of dark hairs that connected her eyebrows there was a marked deepening of that vertical cleft which, visible at all times, warned you that here was a young woman not to be trifled with. Her

brain despatched to her hand a peremptory
message—which miscarried. The spoon wabbled
as though held by a baby. Emily knew that she
herself as a baby had been carried into this very
kitchen to stir the Christmas pudding. Year
after year, as she grew up, she had been allowed
to stir it " for luck." And those, she reflected,
were the only cookery lessons she ever got. How
like Mother!

Mrs. Wrackgarth had died in the past year, of
a complication of ailments.[1] Emily still wore on
her left shoulder that small tag of crape which is
as far as the Five Towns go in the way of
mourning. Her father had died in the year
previous to that, of a still more curious and
enthralling complication of ailments.[2] Jos, his
son, carried on the Wrackgarth Works, and Emily
kept house for Jos. She with her own hand had
made this pudding. But for her this pudding
would not have been. Fantastic! Utterly
incredible! And yet so it was. She was grown-
up. She was mistress of the house. She could
make or unmake puddings at will. And yet she
was Emily Wrackgarth. Which was absurd.

[1] See " The History of Sarah Wrackgarth," pp. 345–482.
[2] See " The History of Sarah Wrackgarth," pp. 231–344.

SCRUTS

She would not try to explain, to reconcile. She abandoned herself to the exquisite mysteries of existence. And yet in her abandonment she kept a sharp look-out on herself, trying fiercely to make head or tail of her nature. She thought herself a fool. But the fact that she thought so was for her a proof of adult sapience. Odd ! She gave herself up. And yet it was just by giving herself up that she seemed to glimpse sometimes her own inwardness. And these bleak revelations saddened her. But she savoured her sadness. It was the wine of life to her. And for her sadness she scorned herself, and in her conscious scorn she recovered her self-respect.

It is doubtful whether the people of southern England have even yet realised how much introspection there is going on all the time in the Five Towns.

Visible from the window of the Wrackgarths' parlour was that colossal statue of Commerce which rears itself aloft at the point where Oodge Lane is intersected by Blackstead Street. Commerce, executed in glossy Doultonware by some sculptor or sculptors unknown, stands pointing her thumb over her shoulder towards the chimneys of far Hanbridge. When I tell you that the circumference of that thumb is six inches, and the rest to scale, you will understand that the statue is one of the prime glories of Bursley. There were times when Emily Wrackgarth seemed to herself as vast and as lustrously impressive as it. There were other times when she seemed to herself as trivial and slavish as one of those performing fleas she had seen at the Annual Ladies' Evening Fête organised by the Bursley Mutual Burial Club. Extremist!

She was now stirring the pudding with her left hand. The ingredients had already been mingled indistinguishably in that rich, undulating mass of tawniness which proclaims perfection. But Emily was determined to give her left hand, not less than her right, what she called "a doing." Emily was like that.

At mid-day, when her brother came home from the Works, she was still at it.

"Brought those scruts with you?" she asked, without looking up.

"That's a fact," he said, dipping his hand into the sagging pocket of his coat.

It is perhaps necessary to explain what scruts are. In the daily output of every potbank there are a certain proportion of flawed vessels. These

are cast aside by the foreman, with a lordly
gesture, and in due course are hammered into
fragments. These fragments, which are put to
various uses, are called scruts; and one of the uses
they are put to is a sentimental one. The dainty
and luxurious Southerner looks to find in his
Christmas pudding a wedding-ring, a gold
thimble, a threepenny-bit, or the like. To
such fal-lals the Five Towns would say fie.
A Christmas pudding in the Five Towns contains
nothing but suet, flour, lemon-peel, cinnamon,
brandy, almonds, raisins—and two or three scruts.
There is a world of poetry, beauty, romance, in
scruts—though you have to have been brought up
on them to appreciate it. Scruts have passed
into the proverbial philosophy of the district.
" Him's a pudden with more scruts than raisins
to 'm " is a criticism not infrequently heard. It
implies respect, even admiration. Of Emily
Wrackgarth herself people often said, in reference
to her likeness to her father, " Her's a scrut o' th'
owd basin."

Jos had emptied out from his pocket on to the
table a good three dozen of scruts. Emily laid
aside her spoon, rubbed the palms of her hands
on the bib of her apron, and proceeded to finger

these scruts with the air of a connoisseur, rejecting one after another. The pudding was a small one, designed merely for herself and Jos, with remainder to " the girl "; so that it could hardly accommodate more than two or three scruts. Emily knew well that one scrut is as good as another. Yet she did not want her brother to feel that anything selected by him would necessarily pass muster with her. For his benefit she ostentatiously wrinkled her nose.

" By the by," said Jos, " you remember Albert Grapp ? I've asked him to step over from Hanbridge and help eat our snack on Christmas Day."

Emily gave Jos one of her looks. " You've asked that Mr. Grapp ? "

" No objection, I hope ? He's not a bad sort. And he's considered a bit of a ladies' man, you know."

She gathered up all the scruts and let them fall in a rattling shower on the exiguous pudding. Two or three fell wide of the basin. These she added.

" Steady on ! " cried Jos. " What's that for ? "

" That's for your guest," replied his sister. " And if you think you're going to palm me off on to him, or on to any other young fellow, you're a fool, Jos Wrackgarth."

The young man protested weakly, but she cut him short.

"Don't think," she said, "I don't know what you've been after, just of late. Cracking up one young sawny and then another on the chance of me marrying him ! I never heard of such goings on. But here I am, and here I'll stay, as sure as my name's Emily Wrackgarth, Jos Wrackgarth ! "

She was the incarnation of the adorably feminine. She was exquisitely vital. She exuded at every pore the pathos of her young undirected force. It is difficult to write calmly about her. For her, in another age, ships would have been launched and cities besieged. But brothers are a race apart, and blind. It is a fact that Jos would have been glad to see his sister " settled "— preferably in one of the other four Towns.

She took up the spoon and stirred vigorously. The scruts grated and squeaked together around the basin, while the pudding feebly wormed its way up among them.

Albert Grapp, ladies' man though he was, was humble of heart. Nobody knew this but himself. Not one of his fellow clerks in Clither's Bank knew it. The general theory in Hanbridge was " Him's got a stiff opinion o' hisself." But this arose from what was really a sign of humility in him. He made the most of himself. He had, for instance, a way of his own in the matter of dressing. He always wore a voluminous frock-coat, with a pair of neatly-striped vicuna trousers, which he placed every night under his mattress, thus preserving in perfection the crease down the centre of each. His collar was of the highest, secured in front with an aluminium stud, to which was attached by a patent loop a natty bow of dove-coloured sateen. He had two caps, one of blue serge, the other of shepherd's plaid. These he wore on alternate days. He wore them in a way of his own—well back from his forehead, so as not to hide his hair, and with the peak behind. The peak made a sort of half-moon over the back of his collar. Through a fault of his tailor, there was a yawning gap between the back of his collar and the collar of his coat. Whenever he shook

his head, the peak of his cap had the look of a
live thing trying to investigate this abyss.   Dimly
aware of the effect, Albert Grapp shook his head
as seldom as possible.

On wet days he wore a mackintosh.   This, as
he did not yet possess a great-coat, he wore also,
but with less glory, on cold days.   He had hoped
there might be rain on Christmas morning.   But
there was no rain.   "Like my luck," he said as
he came out of his lodgings and turned his steps
to that corner of Jubilee Avenue from which
the Hanbridge-Bursley trams start every half-
hour.

Since Jos Wrackgarth had introduced him to
his sister at the Hanbridge Oddfellows' Biennial
Hop, when he danced two quadrilles with her, he
had seen her but once.   He had nodded to her,
Five Towns fashion, and she had nodded back at
him, but with a look that seemed to say "You
needn't nod next time you see me.   I can get
along well enough without your nods."   A frighten-
ing girl !   And yet her brother had since told him
she seemed "a bit gone, like" on him.   Impossible !
He, Albert Grapp, make an impression on the
brilliant Miss Wrackgarth !   Yet she had sent
him a verbal invite to spend Christmas in her own

home. And the time had come. He was on his
way. Incredible that he should arrive! The
tram must surely overturn, or be struck by light-
ning. And yet no! He arrived safely.

The small servant who opened the door gave
him another verbal message from Miss Wrackgarth.
It was that he must wipe his feet " well " on the
mat. In obeying this order he experienced a
thrill of satisfaction he could not account for.
He must have stood shuffling his boots vigorously
for a full minute. This, he told himself, was life.
He, Albert Grapp, was alive. And the world was
full of other men, all alive; and yet, because they
were not doing Miss Wrackgarth's bidding, none
of them really lived. He was filled with a
vague melancholy. But his melancholy pleased
him.

In the parlour he found Jos awaiting him. The
table was laid for three.

"So you're here, are you?" said the host,
using the Five Towns formula. "Emily's in the
kitchen," he added. "Happen she'll be here
directly."

"I hope she's tol-lol-ish?" asked Albert.

"She is," said Jos. "But don't you go saying
that to her. She doesn't care about society airs

and graces. You'll make no headway if you aren't blunt."

"Oh, right you are," said Albert, with the air of a man who knew his way about.

A moment later Emily joined them, still wearing her kitchen apron. "So you're here, are you ?" she said, but did not shake hands. The servant had followed her in with the tray, and the next few seconds were occupied in the disposal of the beef and trimmings.

The meal began, Emily carving. The main thought of a man less infatuated than Albert Grapp would have been "This girl can't cook. And she'll never learn to." The beef, instead of being red and brown, was pink and white. Uneatable beef! And yet he relished it more than anything he had ever tasted. This beef was her own handiwork. Thus it was because she had made it so . . . . He warily refrained from complimenting her, but the idea of a second helping obsessed him.

"Happen I could do with a bit more, like," he said.

Emily hacked off the bit more and jerked it on to the plate he had held out to her.

"Thanks," he said ; and then, as Emily's lip

curled, and Jos gave him a warning kick under the table, he tried to look as if he had said nothing.

Only when the second course came on did he suspect that the meal was a calculated protest against his presence. This a Christmas pudding? The litter of fractured earthenware was hardly held together by the suet and raisins. All his pride of manhood—and there was plenty of pride mixed up with Albert Grapp's humility—dictated a refusal to touch that pudding. Yet he soon found himself touching it, though gingerly, with his spoon and fork.

In the matter of dealing with scruts there are two schools—the old and the new. The old school pushes its head well over its plate and drops the scrut straight from its mouth. The new school emits the scrut into the fingers of its left hand and therewith deposits it on the rim of the plate. Albert noticed that Emily was of the new school. But might she not despise as affectation in him what came natural to herself? On the other hand, if he showed himself as a prop of the old school, might she not set her face the more stringently against him? The chances were that whichever course he took would be the wrong one.

SCRUTS

It was then that he had an inspiration—an idea of the sort that comes to a man once in his life and finds him, likely as not, unable to put it into practice. Albert was not sure he could consummate this idea of his. He had indisputably fine teeth—" a proper mouthful of grinders" in local phrase. But would they stand the strain he was going to impose on them ? He could but try them. Without a sign of nervousness he raised his spoon, with one scrut in it, to his mouth. This scrut he put between two of his left-side molars, bit hard on it, and—eternity of that moment !—felt it and heard it snap in two. Emily also heard it. He was conscious that at sound of the percussion she started forward and stared at him. But he did not look at her. Calmly, systematically, with gradually diminishing crackles, he reduced that scrut to powder, and washed the powder down with a sip of beer. While he dealt with the second scrut he talked to Jos about the Borough Council's proposal to erect an electric power-station on the site of the old gas-works down Hillport way. He was aware of a slight abrasion inside his left cheek. No matter. He must be more careful. There were six scruts still to be negotiated. He knew that what he

was doing was a thing grandiose, unique, epical ;
a history-making thing ; a thing that would out-
live marble and the gilded monuments of princes.
Yet he kept his head. He did not hurry, nor did
he dawdle. Scrut by scrut, he ground slowly but
he ground exceeding small. And while he did so
he talked wisely and well. He passed from the
power-station to a first edition of Leconte
de Lisle's " Parnasse Contemporain " that he had
picked up for sixpence in Liverpool, and thence
to the Midland's proposal to drive a tunnel under
the Knype Canal so as to link up the main-line
with the Critchworth and Suddleford loop-line.
Jos was too amazed to put in a word. Jos sat
merely gaping—a gape that merged by imper-
ceptible degrees into a grin. Presently he ceased
to watch his guest. He sat watching his sister.

Not once did Albert himself glance in her
direction. She was just a dim silhouette on the
outskirts of his vision. But there she was,
unmoving, and he could feel the fixture of her
unseen eyes. The time was at hand when he
would have to meet those eyes. Would he flinch ?
Was he master of himself ?

The last scrut was powder. No temporising !
He jerked his glass to his mouth. A moment

later, holding out his plate to her, he looked
Emily full in the eyes. They were Emily's eyes,
but not hers alone. They were collective eyes—
that was it ! They were the eyes of stark, staring
womanhood. Her face had been dead white, but
now suddenly up from her throat, over her cheeks,
through the down between her eyebrows, went a
rush of colour, up over her temples, through the
very parting of her hair.

"Happen," he said without a quaver in his
voice, "I'll have a bit more, like."

She flung her arms forward on the table and
buried her face in them. It was a gesture wild
and meek. It was the gesture foreseen and yet
incredible. It was recondite, inexplicable, and
yet obvious. It was the only thing to be done—
and yet, by gum, she had done it.

Her brother had risen from his seat and was
now at the door. "Think I'll step round to the
Works," he said, "and see if they banked up that
furnace aright."

NOTE.—*The author has in preparation a series of volumes
dealing with the life of Albert and Emily Grapp.*

ENDEAVOUR

By

J*HN G*LSW*RTHY

ENDEAVOUR

THE dawn of Christmas Day found London laid out in a shroud of snow. Like a body wasted by diseases that had triumphed over it at last, London lay stark and still now, beneath a sky that was as the closed leaden shell of a coffin. It was what is called an old-fashioned Christmas.

Nothing seemed to be moving except the Thames, whose embanked waters flowed on sullenly in their eternal act of escape to the sea. All along the wan stretch of Cheyne Walk the thin trees stood exanimate, with not a breath of wind to stir the snow that pied their soot-blackened branches. Here and there on the muffled ground lay a sparrow that had been frozen in the night, its little claws sticking up heavenward. But here and there also those tinier adventurers of the London air, smuts, floated vaguely and came to rest on the snow—signs that in the seeming death of civilisation some house-maids at least survived, and some fires had been lit.

A CHRISTMAS GARLAND

One of these fires, crackling in the grate of one of those dining-rooms which look fondly out on the river and tolerantly across to Battersea, was being watched by the critical eye of an aged canary. The cage in which this bird sat was hung in the middle of the bow-window. It contained three perches, and also a pendent hoop. The tray that was its floor had just been cleaned and sanded. In the embrasure to the right was a fresh supply of hemp-seed; in the embrasure to the left the bath-tub had just been refilled with clear water. Stuck between the bars was a large sprig of groundsel. Yet, though all was thus in order, the bird did not eat nor drink, nor did he bathe. With his back to Battersea, and his head sunk deep between his little sloping shoulders, he watched the fire. The windows had for a while been opened, as usual, to air the room for him; and the fire had not yet mitigated the chill. It was not his custom to bathe at so inclement an hour; and his appetite for food and drink, less keen than it had once been, required to be whetted by example—he never broke his fast before his master and mistress broke theirs. Time had been when, for sheer joy in life, he fluttered from perch to perch, though there were none to watch him, and even sang roulades, though there were none to hear. He would not do these things nowadays save at the fond instigation of Mr. and Mrs. Adrian Berridge. The housemaid who ministered to his cage, the parlourmaid who laid the Berridges' breakfast table, sometimes tried to incite him to perform for their own pleasure. But the sense of caste, strong in his protuberant little bosom, steeled him against these advances.

While the breakfast-table was being laid, he heard a faint tap against the window-pane. Turning round, he perceived on the sill a creature like to himself, but very different—a creature who, despite the pretensions of a red waistcoat in the worst possible taste, belonged evidently to the ranks of the outcast and the disinherited. In previous winters the sill had been strewn every morning with bread-crumbs. This winter, no bread-crumbs had been vouchsafed ; and the canary, though he did not exactly understand why this was so, was glad that so it was. He had felt that his poor relations took advantage of the Berridges' kindness. Two or three of them, as pensioners, might not have been amiss. But they came in swarms, and they gobbled their food in a disgusting fashion, not trifling coquettishly with it as birds should. The reason for this, the canary knew, was that they were hungry; and of that he was sorry. He hated to think how much destitution there was in the world; and he could not help thinking about it when samples of it were thrust under his notice. That was the principal reason why he was glad that the window-sill was strewn no more and seldom visited.

He would much rather not have seen this solitary applicant. The two eyes fixed on his made him feel very uncomfortable. And yet, for fear of seeming to be outfaced, he did not like to look away.

The subdued clangour of the gong, sounded for breakfast, gave him an excuse for turning suddenly round and watching the door of the room.

A few moments later there came to him a faint odour of Harris tweed, followed immediately by the short, somewhat stout figure of his master—a man whose mild, fresh, pink, round face seemed to find salvation, as it were, at the last moment, in a neatly-pointed auburn beard.

Adrian Berridge paused on the threshold, as was his wont, with closed eyes and dilated nostrils, enjoying the aroma of complex freshness which the dining-room had at this hour. Pathetically a

ENDEAVOUR

creature of habit, he liked to savour the various
scents, sweet or acrid, that went to symbolise for
him the time and the place. Here were the
immediate scents of dry toast, of China tea, of
napery fresh from the wash, together with that
vague, super-subtle scent which boiled eggs give
out through their unbroken shells. And as a
permanent base to these there was the scent of
much-polished Chippendale, and of bees'-waxed
parquet, and of Persian rugs. To-day, moreover,
crowning the composition, there was the delicate
pungency of the holly that topped the Queen
Anne mirror and the Mantegna prints.

Coming forward into the room, Mr. Berridge
greeted the canary. "Well, Amber, old fellow,"
he said, "a happy Christmas to you!" Affectionately he pushed the tip of a plump white finger
between the bars. "Tweet!" he added.

"Tweet!" answered the bird, hopping to and
fro along his perch.

"Quite an old-fashioned Christmas, Amber!"
said Mr. Berridge, turning to scan the weather.
At sight of the robin, a little spasm of pain con-
tracted his face. A shine of tears came to his
prominent pale eyes, and he turned quickly away.
Just at that moment, heralded by a slight

107

fragrance of old lace and of that peculiar, almost unseizable odour that uncut turquoises have, Mrs. Berridge appeared.

"What is the matter, Adrian?" she asked quickly. She glanced sideways into the Queen Anne mirror, her hand fluttering, like a pale moth, to her hair, which she always wore braided in a fashion she had derived from Pollaiuolo's St. Ursula.

"Nothing, Jacynth—nothing," he answered with a lightness that carried no conviction; and he made behind his back a gesture to frighten away the robin.

"Amber isn't unwell, is he?" She came quickly to the cage. Amber executed for her a roulade of great sweetness. His voice had not perhaps the fullness for which it had been noted in earlier years; but the art with which he managed it was as exquisite as ever. It was clear to his audience that the veteran artist was hale and hearty.

But Jacynth, relieved on one point, had a misgiving on another. "This groundsel doesn't look very fresh, does it?" she murmured, withdrawing the sprig from the bars. She rang the bell, and when the servant came in answer to it

ENDEAVOUR

said, " Oh Jenny, will you please bring up another
piece of groundsel for Master Amber? I don't
think this one is quite fresh."

This formal way of naming the canary to the
servants always jarred on her principles and on
those of her husband. They tried to regard their
servants as essentially equals of themselves, and
lately had given Jenny strict orders to leave off
calling them " Sir " and " Ma'am," and to call them
simply " Adrian " and " Jacynth." But Jenny,
after one or two efforts that ended in faint giggles,
had reverted to the crude old nomenclature—as
much to the relief as to the mortification of the
Berridges. They did, it is true, discuss the
possibility of redressing the balance by calling the
parlourmaid " Miss." But, when it came to
the point, their lips refused this office. And con-
versely their lips persisted in the social prefix to
the bird's name.

Somehow that anomaly seemed to them
symbolic of their lives. Both of them yearned so
wistfully to live always in accordance to the
nature of things. And this, they felt, ought
surely to be the line of least resistance. In the
immense difficulties it presented, and in their
constant failures to surmount these difficulties,

they often wondered whether the nature of things might not be, after all, something other than what they thought it. Again and again it seemed to be in as direct conflict with duty as with inclination ; so that they were driven to wonder also whether what they conceived to be duty were not also a mirage—a marsh-light leading them on to disaster.

The fresh groundsel was brought in while Jacynth was pouring out the tea. She rose and took it to the cage ; and it was then that she too saw the robin, still fluttering on the sill. With a quick instinct she knew that Adrian had seen it— knew what had brought that look to his face. She went and, bending over him, laid a hand on his shoulder. The disturbance of her touch caused the tweed to give out a tremendous volume of scent, making her feel a little dizzy.

" Adrian," she faltered, " mightn't we for once —it is Christmas Day—mightn't we, just to-day, sprinkle some bread-crumbs ? "

He rose from the table, and leaned against the mantelpiece, looking down at the fire. She watched him tensely. At length, " Oh Jacynth," he groaned, " don't—don't tempt me."

" But surely, dear, surely——"

ENDEAVOUR

"Jacynth, don't you remember that long talk we had last winter, after the annual meeting of the Feathered Friends' League, and how we agreed that those sporadic doles could do no real good— must even degrade the birds who received them— and that we had no right to meddle in what ought to be done by collective action of the State ?"

"Yes, and—oh my dear, I do still agree, with all my heart. But if the State will do nothing— nothing——"

"It won't, it daren't, go on doing nothing, unless we encourage it to do so. Don't you see, Jacynth, it is just because so many people take it on themselves to feed a few birds here and there that the State feels it can afford to shirk the responsibility ?"

"All that is fearfully true. But just now— Adrian, the look in that robin's eyes——"

Berridge covered his own eyes, as though to blot out from his mind the memory of that look. But Jacynth was not silenced. She felt herself dragged on by her sense of duty to savour, and to make her husband savour, the full bitterness that the situation could yield for them both. "Adrian," she said, "a fearful thought

111

came to me. Suppose—suppose it had been Amber ! "

Even before he shuddered at the thought, he raised his finger to his lips, glancing round at the cage. It was clear that Amber had not overheard Jacynth's remark, for he threw back his head and uttered one of his blithest trills. Adrian, thus relieved, was free to shudder at the thought just suggested.

"Sometimes," murmured Jacynth, "I wonder if we, holding the views we hold, are justified in keeping Amber."

"Ah, dear, we took him in our individualistic days. We cannot repudiate him now. It wouldn't be fair. Besides, you see, he isn't here on a basis of mere charity. He's not a parasite, but an artist. He gives us of his art."

"Yes, dear, I know. But you remember our doubts about the position of artists in the community—whether the State ought to sanction them at all."

"True. But we cannot visit those doubts on our old friend yonder, can we, dear ? At the same time, I admit that when—when—Jacynth, if ever anything happens to Amber, we shall perhaps not be justified in keeping another bird."

ENDEAVOUR

" Don't, please don't talk of such things." She moved to the window. Snow, a delicate white powder, was falling on the coverlet of snow.

Outside, on the sill, the importunate robin lay supine, his little heart beating no more behind the shabby finery of his breast, but his glazing eyes half-open as though even in death he were still questioning. Above him and all around him brooded the genius of infinity, dispassionate, inscrutable, grey.

Jacynth turned and mutely beckoned her husband to the window.

They stood there, these two, gazing silently down.

Presently Jacynth said : " Adrian, are you sure that we, you and I, for all our theories, and all our efforts, aren't futile ? "

" No, dear. Sometimes I am not sure. But—there's a certain comfort in not being sure. To die for what one knows to be true, as many saints have done—that is well. But to live, as many of us do nowadays, in service of what may, for aught we know, be only a half-truth or not true at all—this seems to me nobler still."

" Because it takes more out of us ? "

" Because it takes more out of us."

113

A CHRISTMAS GARLAND

Standing between the live bird and the dead, they gazed across the river, over the snow-covered wharves, over the dim, slender chimneys from which no smoke came, into the grey-black veil of the distance. And it seemed to them that the genius of infinity did not know—perhaps did not even care—whether they were futile or not, nor how much and to what purpose, if to any purpose, they must go on striving.

CHRISTMAS

By

G. S. STR✶✶T

CHRISTMAS

ONE likes it or not. This said, there is plaguey little else to say of Christmas, and I (though I doubt my sentiments touch you not at all) would rather leave that little unsaid. Did I confess a distaste for Christmas, I should incur your enmity. But if I find it, as I protest I do, rather agreeable than otherwise, why should I spoil my pleasure by stringing vain words about it ? Swift and the broomstick—yes. But that essay was done at the behest of a clever woman, and to annoy the admirers of Robert Boyle. Besides, it was hardly—or do you think it was ?— worth the trouble of doing it. There was no trouble involved ? Possibly. But I am not the Dean. And anyhow the fact that he never did anything of the kind again may be taken to imply that he would not be bothered. So would not I, if I had a deanery.

That is an hypothesis I am tempted to pursue. I should like to fill my allotted space before reaching the tiresome theme I have set myself . . . A deanery, the cawing of rooks, their effect on

the nervous system, Trollope's delineations of
deans, the advantages of the Mid-Victorian
novel . . . But your discursive essayist is a
nuisance. Best come to the point. The bore is
in finding a point to come to. Besides, the
chances are that any such point will have long
ago been worn blunt by a score of more active
seekers. Alas!

Since I wrote the foregoing words, I have been
out for a long walk, in search of inspiration,
through the streets of what is called the West
End. Snobbishly so called. Why draw these
crude distinctions? We all know that Mayfair
happens to lie a few miles further west than
Whitechapel. It argues a lack of breeding to go
on calling attention to the fact. If the people
of Whitechapel were less beautiful or less well-
mannered or more ignorant than we, there might
be some excuse. But they are not so. True,
themselves talk about the East End, but this
only makes the matter worse. To a sensitive ear
their phrase has a ring of ironic humility that
jars not less than our own coarse boastfulness.
Heaven knows they have a right to be ironic, and
who shall blame them for exercising it? All the
same, this sort of thing worries me horribly.

CHRISTMAS

I said that I found Christmas rather agreeable than otherwise. But I was speaking as one accustomed to live mostly in the past. The walk I have just taken, refreshing in itself, has painfully reminded me that I cannot hit it off with the present. My life is in the later days of the eighteenth and the earlier days of the nineteenth century. This twentieth affair is as a vision, dimly foreseen at odd moments, and put from me with a slight shudder. My actual Christmases are spent (say) in Holland House, which has but recently been built. Little Charles Fox is allowed by his father to join us for the earlier stages of dessert. I am conscious of patting him on the head and predicting for him a distinguished future. A very bright little fellow, with his father's eyes! Or again, I am down at Newstead. Byron is in his wildest spirits, a shade too uproarious. I am glad to escape into the park and stroll a quiet hour on the arm of Mr. Hughes Ball. Years pass. The approach of Christmas finds one loth to leave one's usual haunts. One is on one's way to one's club to dine with Postumus and dear old " Wigsby " Pendennis, quietly, at one's consecrated table near the fireplace. As one is crossing St. James's Street an ear-piercing grunt

causes one to reel back just in time to be not run
over by a motor-car. Inside is a woman who
scowls down at one through the window—" Serve
you right if we'd gone over you." Yes, I often
have these awakenings to fact—or rather these
provisions of what life might be if I survived into
the twentieth century. Alas!

I have mentioned that woman in the motor-car
because she is germane to my theme. She
typifies the vices of the modern Christmas. For
her, by the absurd accident of her wealth, there is
no distinction between people who have not
motor-cars and people who might as well be run
over. But I wrong her. If we others were all
run over, there would be no one before whom she
could flaunt her loathsome air of superiority.
And what would she do then, poor thing? I
doubt she would die of boredom—painfully, one
hopes. In the same way, if the shop-keepers in
Bond Street knew there was no one who could
not afford to buy the things in their windows,
there would be an end to the display that makes
those windows intolerable (to you and me) during
the month of December. I had often suspected
that the things there were not meant to be
bought by people who could buy them, but

CHRISTMAS

merely to irritate the rest. This afternoon I was sure of it. Not in one window anything a sane person would give to any one not an idiot, but everywhere a general glossy grin out at people who are not plutocrats. This sort of thing lashes me to ungovernable fury. The lion is roused, and I recognise in myself a born leader of men. Be so good as to smash those windows for me.

One does not like to think that Christmas has been snapped up, docked of its old-world kindliness, and pressed into the service of an odious ostentation. But so it has. Alas ! The thought of Father Christmas trudging through the snow to the homes of gentle and simple alike (forgive that stupid, snobbish phrase) was agreeable. But Father Christmas in red plush breeches, lounging on the doorstep of Sir Gorgius Midas—one averts one's eyes.

I have—now I come to think of it—another objection to the modern Christmas. It would be affectation to pretend not to know that there are many Jews living in England, and in London especially. I have always had a deep respect for that race, their distinction in intellect and in character. Being not one of them, I may in their behalf put a point which themselves would be the

121

last to suggest. I hope they will acquit me of
impertinence in doing this. You, in your turn,
must acquit me of sentimentalism. The Jews are
a minority, and as such must take their chances.
But may not a majority refrain from pressing its
rights to the utmost? It is well that we should
celebrate Christmas heartily, and all that. But
we could do so without an emphasis that seems to
me, in the circumstances, 'tother side good taste.
"Good taste" is a hateful phrase. But it escaped
me in the heat of the moment. Alas!

THE FEAST

By

J*S*PH C*NR*D

THE FEAST

THE hut in which slept the white man was on a clearing between the forest and the river. Silence, the silence murmurous and unquiet of a tropical night, brooded over the hut that, baked through by the sun, sweated a vapour beneath the cynical light of the stars. Mahamo lay rigid and watchful at the hut's mouth. In his upturned eyes, and along the polished surface of his lean body black and immobile, the stars were reflected, creating an illusion of themselves who are illusions.

The roofs of the congested trees, writhing in some kind of agony private and eternal, made tenebrous and shifty silhouettes against the sky, like shapes cut out of black paper by a maniac who pushes them with his thumb this way and that, irritably, on a concave surface of blue steel. Resin oozed unseen from the upper branches to the trunks swathed in creepers that clutched and interlocked with tendrils venomous, frantic and faint. Down below, by force of habit, the lush herbage went through the farce of growth—that

125

farce old and screaming, whose trite end is decomposition.

Within the hut the form of the white man, corpulent and pale, was covered with a mosquito-net that was itself illusory like everything else, only more so. Flying squadrons of mosquitoes inside its meshes flickered and darted over him, working hard, but keeping silence so as not to excite him from sleep. Cohorts of yellow ants disputed him against cohorts of purple ants, the two kinds slaying one another in thousands. The battle was undecided when suddenly, with no such warning as it gives in some parts of the world, the sun blazed up over the horizon, turning night into day, and the insects vanished back into their camps.

The white man ground his knuckles into the corners of his eyes, emitting that snore final and querulous of a middle-aged man awakened rudely. With a gesture brusque but flaccid he plucked aside the net and peered around. The bales of cotton cloth, the beads, the brass wire, the bottles of rum, had not been spirited away in the night. So far so good. The faithful servant of his employers was now at liberty to care for his own interests. He regarded himself, passing his hands over his skin.

126

THE FEAST

"Hi! Mahamo!" he shouted. "I've been eaten up."

The islander, with one sinuous motion, sprang from the ground, through the mouth of the hut. Then, after a glance, he threw high his hands in thanks to such good and evil spirits as had charge of his concerns. In a tone half of reproach, half of apology, he murmured—

"You white men sometimes say strange things that deceive the heart."

"Reach me that ammonia bottle, d'you hear?" answered the white man. "This is a pretty place you've brought me to!" He took a draught. "Christmas Day, too! Of all the—— But I suppose it seems all right to you, you funny blackamoor, to be here on Christmas Day?"

"We are here on the day appointed, Mr. Williams. It is a feast-day of your people?"

Mr. Williams had lain back, with closed eyes, on his mat. Nostalgia was doing duty to him for imagination. He was wafted to a bedroom in Marylebone, where in honour of the Day he lay late dozing, with great contentment; outside, a slush of snow in the street, the sound of church-bells; from below a savour of especial cookery.

"Yes," he said, "it's a feast-day of my people."

"Of mine also," said the islander humbly.

"Is it though? But they'll do business first?"

"They must first do that."

"And they'll bring their ivory with them?"

"Every man will bring ivory," answered the islander, with a smile gleaming and wide.

"How soon'll they be here?"

"Has not the sun risen? They are on their way."

"Well, I hope they'll hurry. The sooner we're off this cursed island of yours the better. Take all those things out," Mr. Williams added, pointing to the merchandise, "and arrange them— neatly, mind you!"

In certain circumstances it is right that a man be humoured in trifles. Mahamo, having borne out the merchandise, arranged it very neatly.

While Mr. Williams made his toilet, the sun and the forest, careless of the doings of white and black men alike, waged their warfare implacable and daily. The forest from its inmost depths sent forth perpetually its legions of shadows that fell dead in the instant of exposure to the enemy

whose rays heroic and absurd its outposts anni-
hilated. There came from those inilluminable
depths the equable rumour of myriads of winged
things and crawling things newly roused to the
task of killing and being killed. Thence detached
itself, little by little, an insidious sound of a
drum beaten. This sound drew more near.

Mr. Williams, issuing from the hut, heard it, and
stood gaping towards it.

" Is that them ? " he asked.

" That is they," the islander murmured, moving
away towards the edge of the forest.

Sounds of chanting were a now audible ac-
companiment to the drum.

" What's that they're singing ? " asked Mr.
Williams.

" They sing of their business," said Mahamo.

"Oh !" Mr. Williams was slightly shocked. " I'd
have thought they'd be singing of their feast."

" It is of their feast they sing."

It has been stated that Mr. Williams was not
imaginative. But a few years of life in climates
alien and intemperate had disordered his nerves.
There was that in the rhythms of the hymn which
made bristle his flesh.

Suddenly, when they were very near, the voices

ceased, leaving a legacy of silence more sinister than themselves. And now the black spaces between the trees were relieved by bits of white that were the eyeballs and teeth of Mahamo's brethren.

"It was of their feast, it was of you, they sang," said Mahamo.

"Look here," cried Mr. Williams in his voice of a man not to be trifled with. "Look here, if you've——"

He was silenced by sight of what seemed to be a young sapling sprung up from the ground within a yard of him—a young sapling tremulous, with a root of steel. Then a thread-like shadow skimmed the air, and another spear came imping- ing the ground within an inch of his feet.

As he turned in his flight he saw the goods so neatly arranged at his orders, and there flashed through him, even in the thick of the spears, the thought that he would be a grave loss to his employers. This—for Mr. Williams was, not less than the goods, of a kind easily replaced—was an illusion. It was the last of Mr. Williams' illusions.

A RECOLLECTION

By

EDM✶ND G✶SSE

A RECOLLECTION

"And let us strew
Twain wreaths of holly and of yew."

WALLER.

ONE out of many Christmas Days abides with peculiar vividness in my memory. In setting down, however clumsily, some slight record of it, I feel that I shall be discharging a duty not only to the two disparately illustrious men who made it so very memorable, but also to all young students of English and Scandinavian literature. My use of the first person singular, delightful though that pronoun is in the works of the truly gifted, jars unspeakably on me ; but reasons of space baulk my sober desire to call myself merely the present writer, or the infatuated go-between, or the cowed and imponderable young person who was in attendance.

In the third week of December, 1878, taking the opportunity of a brief and undeserved vacation, I went to Venice. On the morning after my arrival, in answer to a most kind and cordial summons, I presented myself at the Palazzo

Rezzonico. Intense as was the impression he always made even in London, I think that those of us who met Robert Browning only in the stress and roar of that metropolis can hardly have gauged the fullness of his potentialities for impressing. Venice, "so weak, so quiet," as Mr. Ruskin had called her, was indeed the ideal setting for one to whom neither of those epithets could by any possibility have been deemed applicable. The steamboats that now wake the echoes of the canals had not yet been imported; but the vitality of the imported poet was in some measure a preparation for them. It did not, however, find me quite prepared for itself, and I am afraid that some minutes must have elapsed before I could, as it were, find my feet in the torrent of his geniality and high spirits, and give him news of his friends in London.

He was at that time engaged in revising the proof-sheets of " Dramatic Idylls," and after luncheon, to which he very kindly bade me remain, he read aloud certain selected passages. The yellow haze of a wintry Venetian sunshine poured in through the vast windows of his *salone*, making an aureole around his silvered head. I would give much to live that hour over again. But it

A RECOLLECTION

was vouchsafed in days before the Browning
Society came and made everything so simple for
us all. I am afraid that after a few minutes I sat
enraptured by the sound rather than by the sense
of the lines. I find, in the notes I made of the
occasion, that I figured myself as plunging through
some enchanted thicket on the back of an inspired
bull.

That evening, as I was strolling in Piazza San
Marco, my thoughts of Browning were all of a
sudden scattered by the vision of a small, thick-set
man seated at one of the tables in the Café
Florian. This was—and my heart leapt like a
young trout when I saw that it could be none
other than—Henrik Ibsen. Whether joy or fear
was the predominant emotion in me, I should be
hard put to it to say. It had been my privilege to
correspond extensively with the great Scandinavian,
and to be frequently received by him, some years
earlier than the date of which I write, in Rome.
In that city haunted by the shades of so many
Emperors and Popes I had felt comparatively at
ease even in Ibsen's presence. But seated here in
the homelier decay of Venice, closely buttoned in
his black surcoat and crowned with his uncom-
promising top-hat, with the lights of the Piazza

flashing back wanly from his gold-rimmed
spectacles, and his lips tight-shut like some steel
trap into which our poor humanity had just fallen,
he seemed to constitute a menace under which the
boldest might well quail. Nevertheless, I took my
courage in both hands, and laid it as a kind of
votive offering on the little table before him.

My reward was in the surprising amiability that
he then and afterwards displayed. My travelling
had indeed been doubly blessed, for, whilst my
subsequent afternoons were spent in Browning's
presence, my evenings fell with regularity into
the charge of Ibsen. One of these evenings is for me
" prouder, more laurel'd than the rest " as having
been the occasion when he read to me the MS. of
a play which he had just completed. He was
staying at the Hôtel Danieli, an edifice famous
for having been, rather more than forty years
previously, the socket in which the flame of an
historic *grande passion* had finally sunk and
guttered out with no inconsiderable accompani-
ment of smoke and odour. It was there, in an
upper room, that I now made acquaintance with
a couple very different from George Sand and
Alfred de Musset, though destined to become
hardly less famous than they. I refer to Torvald

and Nora Helmer. My host read to me with the
utmost vivacity, standing in the middle of the
apartment ; and I remember that in the scene
where Nora Helmer dances the tarantella her
creator instinctively executed a few illustrative
steps.

During those days I felt very much as might a
minnow swimming to and fro between Leviathan
on the one hand and Behemoth on the other—a
minnow tremulously pleased, but ever wistful for
some means of bringing his two enormous
acquaintances together. On the afternoon of
December 24th I confided to Browning my
aspiration. He had never heard of this brother
poet and dramatist, whose fame indeed was at
that time still mainly Boreal ; but he cried out
with the greatest heartiness, "Capital! Bring him
round with you at one o'clock to-morrow for
turkey and plum-pudding ! "

I betook myself straight to the Hôtel Danieli,
hoping against hope that Ibsen's sole answer
would not be a comminatory grunt and an instant
rupture of all future relations with myself. At
first he was indeed resolute not to go. He had never
heard of this Herr Browning. (It was one of the
strengths of his strange, crustacean genius that

he never had heard of anybody.) I took it on
myself to say that Herr Browning would send his
private gondola, propelled by his two gondoliers,
to conduct Herr Ibsen to the scene of the festivity.
I think it was this prospect that made him
gradually unbend, for he had already acquired
that taste for pomp and circumstance which was
so notable a characteristic of his later years. I
hastened back to the Palazzo Rezzonico before he
could change his mind. I need hardly say that
Browning instantly consented to send the gondola.
So large and lovable was his nature that, had he
owned a thousand of those conveyances, he would
not have hesitated to send out the whole fleet in
honour of any friend of any friend of his.

Next day, as I followed Ibsen down the
Danielian water-steps into the expectant gondola,
my emotion was such that I was tempted to
snatch from him his neatly-furled umbrella and
spread it out over his head, like the umbrella
beneath which the Doges of days gone by had
made their appearances in public. It was perhaps
a pity that I repressed this impulse. Ibsen seemed
to be already regretting that he had unbent. I
could not help thinking, as we floated along the
Riva Schiavoni, that he looked like some par-

ticularly ruthless member of the Council of Ten.
I did, however, try faintly to attune him in some
sort to the spirit of our host and of the day of
the year. I adumbrated Browning's outlook on
life, translating into Norwegian, I well remember,
the words " God's in His heaven, all's right with
the world." In fact I cannot charge myself with
not having done what I could. I can only lament
that it was not enough.

When we marched into the *salone*, Browning
was seated at the piano, playing (I think) a
Toccata of Galuppi's. On seeing us, he brought
his hands down with a great crash on the key-
board, seemed to reach us in one astonishing bound
across the marble floor, and clapped Ibsen loudly
on either shoulder, wishing him " the Merriest of
Merry Christmases."

Ibsen, under this sudden impact, stood firm as
a rock, and it flitted through my brain that here
at last was solved the old problem of what would
happen if an irresistible force met an immoveable
mass. But it was obvious that the rock was not
rejoicing in the moment of victory. I was tartly
asked whether I had not explained to Herr
Browning that his guest did not understand
English. I hastily rectified my omission, and

A CHRISTMAS GARLAND

thenceforth our host spoke in Italian. Ibsen,
though he understood that language fairly well,
was averse to speaking it. Such remarks as he
made in the course of the meal to which we presently sat down were made in Norwegian and
translated by myself.

Browning, while he was carving the turkey,
asked Ibsen whether he had visited any of the
Venetian theatres. Ibsen's reply was that he
never visited theatres. Browning laughed his
great laugh, and cried "That's right! We poets
who write plays must give the theatres as wide a
berth as possible. We aren't wanted there!"
"How so?" asked Ibsen. Browning looked a
little puzzled, and I had to explain that in
northern Europe Herr Ibsen's plays were frequently performed. At this I seemed to see on
Browning's face a slight shadow—so swift and
transient a shadow as might be cast by a swallow
flying across a sunlit garden. An instant, and it
was gone. I was glad, however, to be able to
soften my statement by adding that Herr Ibsen
had in his recent plays abandoned the use of
verse.

The trouble was that in Browning's company
he seemed practically to have abandoned the use

140

A RECOLLECTION

of prose too. When, moreover, he did speak, it
was always in a sense contrary to that of our host.
The Risorgimento was a theme always very near
to the great heart of Browning, and on this
occasion he hymned it with more than his usual
animation and resource (if indeed that were possible). He descanted especially on the vast
increase that had accrued to the sum of human
happiness in Italy since the success of that remarkable movement. When Ibsen rapped out
the conviction that what Italy needed was to be
invaded and conquered once and for all by
Austria, I feared that an explosion was inevitable.
But hardly had my translation of the inauspicious
sentiment been uttered when the plum-pudding
was borne into the room, flaming on its dish. I
clapped my hands wildly at sight of it, in the
English fashion, and was intensely relieved when
the yet more resonant applause of Robert
Browning followed mine. Disaster had been
averted by a crowning mercy. But I am afraid
that Ibsen thought us both quite mad.

The next topic that was started, harmless
though it seemed at first, was fraught with yet
graver peril. The world of scholarship was at
that time agitated by the recent discovery of

what might or might not prove to be a fragment of Sappho. Browning proclaimed his unshakeable belief in the authenticity of these verses. To my surprise, Ibsen, whom I had been unprepared to regard as a classical scholar, said positively that they had not been written by Sappho. Browning challenged him to give a reason. A literal translation of the reply would have been " Because no woman ever was capable of writing a fragment of good poetry." Imagination reels at the effect this would have had on the recipient of " Sonnets from the Portuguese." The agonised interpreter, throwing honour to the winds, babbled some wholly fallacious version of the words. Again the situation had been saved ; but it was of the kind that does not even in furthest retrospect lose its power to freeze the heart and constrict the diaphragm.

I was fain to thank heaven when, immediately after the termination of the meal, Ibsen rose, bowed to his host, and bade me express his thanks for the entertainment. Out on the Grand Canal, in the gondola which had again been placed at our disposal, his passion for " documents " that might bear on his work was quickly manifested. He asked me whether Herr

A RECOLLECTION

Browning had ever married. Receiving an emphatically affirmative reply, he inquired whether Fru Browning had been happy. Loth though I was to cast a blight on his interest in the matter, I conveyed to him with all possible directness the impression that Elizabeth Barrett had assuredly been one of those wives who do not dance tarantellas nor slam front-doors. He did not, to the best of my recollection, make further mention of Browning, either then or afterwards. Browning himself, however, thanked me warmly, next day, for having introduced my friend to him. " A capital fellow ! " he exclaimed, and then, for a moment, seemed as though he were about to qualify this estimate, but ended by merely repeating " A capital fellow ! "

Ibsen remained in Venice some weeks after my return to London. He was, it may be conjectured, bent on a specially close study of the Bride of the Adriatic because her marriage had been not altogether a happy one. But there appears to be no evidence whatsoever that he went again, either of his own accord or by invitation, to the Palazzo Rezzonico.

143

OF CHRISTMAS
By
H*L**RE B*LL*C

OF CHRISTMAS

THERE was a man came to an Inn by night, and after he had called three times they should open him the door—though why three times, and not three times three, nor thirty times thirty, which is the number of the little stone devils that make mows at St. Aloesius of Ledera over against the marshes Gué-la-Nuce to this day, nor three hundred times three hundred (which is a bestial number), nor three thousand times three-and-thirty, upon my soul I know not, and nor do you —when, then, this jolly fellow had three times cried out, shouted, yelled, holloa'd, loudly besought, caterwauled, brayed, sung out, and roared, he did by the same token set himself to beat, hammer, bang, pummel, and knock at the door. Now the door was Oak. It had been grown in the forest of Boulevoise, hewn in Barre-le-Neuf, seasoned in South Hoxton, hinged nowhere in particular, and panelled—and that most abominably well—in Arque, where the peasants sell their souls for skill in such handi-craft. But our man knew nothing of all this, which, had he known it, would have mattered little enough to him, for a reason which I propose to tell in the next sentence. The door was opened. As to the reasons why it was not opened sooner, these are most tediously set forth in Professor Sir T. K. Slibby's " Half-Hours With Historic Doors," as also in a fragment at one time attributed to Oleaginus Silo but now proven a forgery by Miss Evans. Enough for our purpose, merry reader of mine, that the door was opened.

The man, as men will, went in. And there, for God's sake and by the grace of Mary Mother, let us leave him ; for the truth of it is that his strength was all in his lungs, and himself a poor, weak, clout-faced, wizen-bellied, pin-shanked bloke anyway, who at Trinity Hall had spent the most of his time in reading Hume (that was Satan's lackey) and after taking his degree did a little in the way of Imperial Finance. Of him it was that Lord Abraham Hart, that far-seeing statesman, said, " This young man has the root of the matter in him." I quote the epigram rather for its perfect form than for its truth. For once, Lord Abraham was deceived. But it must be remembered that he was at this time being plagued almost out of his wits by the vile (though cleverly engineered) agitation for the compulsory winding-up of the Rondoosdop Development Company. Afterwards, in Wormwood Scrubbs, his Lordship admitted that his estimate of his young friend had perhaps been pitched too high. In Dartmoor he has since revoked it altogether, with that manliness for which the Empire so loved him when he was at large.

Now the young man's name was Dimby—"Trot" Dimby—and his mother had been a Clupton, so that—but had I not already dismissed him? Indeed I only mentioned him because it seemed that his going to that Inn might put me on track of that One Great Ultimate and Final True Thing I am purposed to say about Christmas. Don't ask me yet what that Thing is. Truth dwells in no man, but is a shy beast you must hunt as you may in the forests that are round about the Walls of Heaven. And I do hereby curse, gibbet, and denounce *in execrationem perpetuam atque aeternam* the man who hunts in a crafty or calculating way—as, lying low, nosing for scents, squinting for trails, crawling noise-lessly till he shall come near to his quarry and

then taking careful aim.   Here's to him who
hunts Truth in the honest fashion of men, which
is, going blindly at it, following his first scent (if
such there be) or (if none) none, scrambling over
boulders, fording torrents, winding his horn,
plunging into thickets, skipping, firing off his gun
in the air continually, and then ramming in some
more ammunition anyhow, with a laugh and a
curse if the charge explode in his own jolly face.
The chances are he will bring home in his bag
nothing but a field-mouse he trod on by accident.
Not the less his is the true sport and the essential
stuff of holiness.

As touching Christmas—but there is nothing
like verse to clear the mind, heat the blood,
and make very humble the heart.   Rouse thee,
Muse !

One Christmas Night in Pontgibaud
    (*Pom-pom, rub-a-dub-dub*)
A man with a drum went to and fro
    (*Two merry eyes, two cheeks chub*)
Nor not a citril within, without,
But heard the racket and heard the rout
And marvelled what it was all about
    (*And who shall shrive Beelzebub ?*)

OF CHRISTMAS

He whacked so hard the drum was split
    (*Pom-pom, rub-a-dub-dum*)
Out lept Saint Gabriel from it
    (*Praeclarissimus Omnium*)
Who spread his wings and up he went
Nor ever paused in his ascent
Till he had reached the firmament
    (*Benedicamus Dominum*).

That's what I shall sing (please God) at dawn
to-morrow, standing on the high, green barrow at
Storrington, where the bones of Athelstan's men
are.   Yea,

At dawn to-morrow
  On Storrington Barrow
I'll beg or borrow
  A bow and arrow
And shoot sleek sorrow
  Through the marrow.
The floods are out and the ford is narrow,
The stars hang dead and my limbs are lead,
  But ale is gold
  And there's good foot-hold
On the Cuckfield side of Storrington Barrow.

This too I shall sing, and other songs that are

151

yet to write. In Pagham I shall sing them again, and again in Little Dewstead. In Hornside I shall rewrite them, and at the Scythe and Turtle in Liphook (if I have patience) annotate them. At Selsey they will be very damnably in the way, and I don't at all know what I shall do with them at Selsey.

Such then, as I see it, is the whole pith, mystery, outer form, common acceptation, purpose, usage usual, meaning and inner meaning, beauty intrinsic and extrinsic, and right character of Christmas Feast. *Habent urbs atque orbis revelationem.* Pray for my soul.

A STRAIGHT TALK

By

G**RGE B*RN*RD SH*W

A STRAIGHT TALK

(Preface to " Snt George : A Christmas Play.")

WHEN a public man lays his hand on his heart and declares that his conduct needs no apology, the audience hastens to put up its umbrellas against the particularly severe downpour of apologies in store for it. I wont give the customary warning. My conduct shrieks aloud for apology, and you are in for a thorough drenching.

Flatly, I stole this play. The one valid excuse for the theft would be mental starvation. That excuse I shant plead. I could have made a dozen better plays than this out of my own head. You dont suppose Shakespeare was so vacant in the upper storey that there was nothing for it but to rummage through cinquecento romances, Townley Mysteries, and suchlike insanitary rubbishheaps, in order that he might fish out enough scraps for his artistic fangs to fasten on. Depend on it, there were plenty of decent original notions seething behind yon marble brow. Why didn't our William use t h e m ? He was too lazy. And so am I. It is easier to give a new twist to somebody else's story that you take readymade than to perform that highly-specialised form of skilled labor which consists in giving artistic coherence to a story that you have conceived roughly for yourself. A literary gentleman once hoisted a theory that there are only thirty-six possible stories in the world. This—I say it with no deference at all—is bosh. There are as many possible stories in the world as there are microbes in the well-lined shelves of a literary gentleman's "den." On the other hand, it is perfectly true that only a baker's dozen of these have got themselves told. The reason lies in that bland, unalterable resolve to shirk honest work, by which you recognise the artist as surely as you recognise the leopard by his spots. In so far as I am an artist, I am a loafer. And if you expect me, in that line, to do anything but loaf, you will get the shock your romantic folly deserves. The only difference between me and my rivals past and present is that I have the decency to be ashamed of myself. So that if you are not too bemused and bedevilled by my "brilliancy" to kick me downstairs, you may rely on me to cheerfully lend a foot in the operation. But, while I have my share of judicial vindictiveness against crime, Im not going to talk the common judicial cant about brutality making a Better Man of the criminal. I havent the slightest doubt that I would thieve again at the earliest opportunity. Meanwhile be so good as to listen to the evidence on the present charge.

In the December after I was first cast ashore at Holyhead, I had to go down to Dorsetshire. In those days the more enterprising farm-laborers used still to annually dress themselves up in order to tickle the gentry into disbursing the money needed to supplement a local-minimum wage. They called themselves the Christmas Mummers, and performed a play entitled Snt George. As my education had been of the typical Irish kind, and the ideas on which I had been nourished were precisely the ideas that once in Tara's Hall were regarded as dangerous novelties, Snt George staggered me with the sense of being suddenly bumped up against a thing which lay centuries ahead of the time I had been born into. (Being, in point of fact, only a matter of five hundred years old, it would have the same effect to-day on the average London playgoer if it was produced

in a west end theatre.) The plot was simple. It
is set forth in Thomas Hardy's "Return of the
Native"; but, as the people who read my books
have no energy left over to cope with other authors,
I must supply an outline of it myself.

Entered, first of all, the English Knight, announc-
ing his determination to fight and vanquish the
Turkish Knight, a vastly superior swordsman, who
promptly made mincemeat of him. After the
Saracen had celebrated his victory in verse, and
proclaimed himself the world's champion, entered
Snt George, who, after some preliminary patriotic
flourishes, promptly made mincemeat of the
Saracen—to the blank amazement of an audience
which included several retired army officers. Snt
George, however, saved his face by the usual expe-
dient of the victorious British general, attributing
to Providence a result which by no polite stretch
of casuistry could have been traced to the opera-
tions of his own brain. But here the dramatist
was confronted by another difficulty: there being
no curtain to ring down, how were the two corpses
to be got gracefully rid of? Entered therefore
the Physician, and brought them both to life. (Any
one objecting to this scene on the score of romantic
improbability is hereby referred to the Royal

A STRAIGHT TALK

College of Physicians, or to the directors of any accredited medical journal, who will hail with delight this opportunity of proving once and for all that re-vitalisation is the child's-play of the Faculty.)

Such then is the play that I have stolen.   For all the many pleasing esthetic qualities you will find in it—dramatic inventiveness, humor and pathos, eloquence, elfin glamor and the like—you must bless the original author : of these things I have only the usufruct.   To me the play owes nothing but the stiffening of civistic conscience that has been crammed in.   Modest ?   Not a bit of it.   It is my civistic conscience that makes a man of me and (incidentally) makes this play a masterpiece.

Nothing could have been easier for me (if I were some one else) than to perform my task in that God-rest-you-merry- gentlemen -may-nothing-you-dismay spirit which so grossly flatters the sensibilities of the average citizen by its assumption that he is sharp enough to be dismayed by what stares him in the face.   Charles Dickens had lucid intervals in which he was vaguely conscious of the abuses around him ; but his spasmodic efforts to expose these brought him into contact with

realities so agonising to his highstrung literary
nerves that he invariably sank back into debauches
of unsocial optimism.   Even the Swan of Avon
had his glimpses of the havoc of displacement
wrought by Elizabethan romanticism in the social
machine which had been working with tolerable
smoothness under   the   prosaic guidance of
Henry 8. The time was out of joint ; and the
Swan, recognising that he was the last person to
ever set it right, consoled himself by offering the
world a soothing doctrine of despair.   Not for
m e, thank you, that Swansdown pillow.   I refuse
as flatly to fuddle myself in the shop of " W.
Shakespeare, Druggist," as to stimulate myself with
the juicy joints of " C. Dickens, Family Butcher."
Of these and suchlike pernicious establishments
my patronage consists in weaving round the shop-
door a barbed-wire entanglement of dialectic and
then training my moral   machine-guns on the
customers.

In this devilish function I have, as you know, acquired by practice a tremendous technical skill ;
and but for the more or less innocent pride I take
in showing off my accomplishment to all and sundry,
I doubt whether even m y iron nerves would be
proof against the horrors that have impelled me to

thus perfect myself. In my nonage I believed humanity could be reformed if only it were intelligently preached at for a sufficiently long period. This first fine careless rapture I could no more recapture, at my age, than I could recapture hoopingcough or nettlerash. One by one, I have flung all political nostra overboard, till there remain only dynamite and scientific breeding. My touching faith in these saves me from pessimism : I believe in the future ; but this only makes the present—which I foresee as going strong for a couple of million of years or so—all the more excruciating by contrast.

For casting into dramatic form a compendium of my indictments of the present from a purely political standpoint, the old play of Snt George occurred to me as having exactly the framework I needed. In the person of the Turkish Knight I could embody that howling chaos which does duty among us for a body-politic. The English Knight would accordingly be the Liberal Party, whose efforts (whenever it is in favor with the electorate) to reduce chaos to order by emulating in foreign politics the blackguardism of a Metternich or Bismarck, and in home politics the spirited attitudinisings of a Garibaldi or Cavor, are foredoomed

A CHRISTMAS GARLAND

to the failure which its inherent oldmaidishness
must always win for the Liberal Party in all under-
takings whatsoever. Snt George is, of course,
myself. But here my very aptitude in controversy
tripped me up as playwright. Owing to my nack
of going straight to the root of the matter in hand
and substituting, before you can say Jack
Robinson, a truth for every fallacy and a natural
law for every convention, the scene of Snt George
(Bernard Shaw)'s victory over the Turkish Knight
came out too short for theatrical purposes. I
calculated that the play as it stood would not
occupy more than five hours in performance. I
therefore departed from the original scheme so far
as to provide the Turkish Knight with three
attendant monsters, severally named the Good, the
Beyootiful, and the Ter-rew, and representing in
themselves the current forms of Religion, Art,
and Science. These three Snt George successively
challenges, tackles, and flattens out—the first as
lunacy, the second as harlotry, the third as witch-
craft. But even so the play would not be long
enough had I not padded a good deal of buffoon-
ery into the scene where the five corpses are
brought back to life.

The restorative Physician symbolises that

A STRAIGHT TALK

irresistible force of human stupidity by which the
rottenest and basest institutions are enabled to
thrive in the teeth of the logic that has demolished
them.   Thus, for the author, the close of the play
is essentially tragic.   But what is death to him is
fun to you, and my buffooneries wont offend any
of you.   Bah !

FOND HEARTS ASKEW

By

M**R*CE H*WL*TT

FOND HEARTS ASKEW

To
William Robertson Nicoll
Sage and Reverend
And a True Knight
This Romaunt
Of Days Edvardian

Prologue.

TOO strong a wine, belike, for some stomachs, for there's honey in it, and a dibbet of gore, with other condiments. Yet Mistress Clio (with whom, some say, Mistress Thalia, that sweet hoyden) brewed it : she, not I, who do but hand the cup round by her warrant and good favour. Her guests, not mine, you shall take it or leave it—spill it untasted or quaff a bellyful. Of a hospitable temper, she whose page I am ; but a great lady, over self-sure to be dudgeoned by wry faces in the refectory. As for the little sister (if she did have finger in the concoction)—no fear of offence there ! I dare vow, who know somewhat the fashion of her, she will but trill a pretty titter or so at your qualms.

A CHRISTMAS GARLAND

I cry you mercy for a lacuna at the outset. I
know not what had knitted and blackened the
brows of certain two speeding eastward through
London, enhansomed, on the night of the feast of
St. Box: *alter*, Geoffrey Dizzard, called "The
Honourable," *lieu-tenant* in the Guards of Edward
the Peace Getter; *altera*, the Lady Angelica
Plantagenet, to him affianced. Devil take the
cause of the bicker: enough that they were at
sulks. Here's for a sight of the girl!

Johannes Sargent, that swift giant from the
New World, had already flung her on canvas,
with a brace of sisters. She outstands there, a
virgin poplar-tall; hair like ravelled flax and
coiffed in the fashion of the period; neck like a
giraffe's; lips shaped for kissing rather than
smiling; eyes like a giraffe's again; breasts like a
boy's, and something of a dressed-up boy in the
total aspect of her. She has arms a trifle long
even for such height as hers; fingers very long,
too, with red-pink nails trimmed to a point. She
looks out slantwise, conscious of her beauty, and
perhaps of certain other things. Fire under that
ice, I conjecture—red corpuscles rampant behind

168

that meek white mask of hers. *"Forsitan in hoc anno pulcherrima debutantium"* is the verdict of a contemporary journal. For *"forsitan"* read *"certe."* No slur, that, on the rest of the bevy.

Very much as Johannes had seen her did she appear now to the cits, as the cabriolet swung past them. Paramount there, she was still more paramount here. Yet this Geoffrey was not ill-looking. In the secret journal of Mary Jane, serving-wench in the palace of Geoffrey's father (who gat his barony by beer) note is made of his "lovely blue eyes ; complexion like a blush rose ; hands like a girl's ; lips like a girl's again ; yellow curls close cropped ; and for moustachio (so young is he yet) such a shadow as amber might cast on water."

Here, had I my will, I would limn you Mary Jane herself, that parched nymph. Time urges, though. The cabrioleteer thrashes his horse (me with it) to a canter, and plunges into Soho. Some wagon athwart the path gives pause. Angelica, looking about her, bites lip. For this is the street of Wardour, wherein (say all the chronicles most absolutely) she and Geoffrey had first met and plit their troth.

" Methinks," cries she, loud and clear to the wagoner, and pointing finger at Geoffrey, " the Devil must be between your shafts, to make a mock of me in this conjunction, the which is truly of his own doing."

" Sweet madam," says Geoffrey (who was also called " The Ready"), " shall I help harness you at his side ? Though, for my part, I doubt 'twere supererogant, in that he buckled you to his service or ever the priest dipped you."

A bitter jest, this ; and the thought of it still tingled on the girl's cheek and clawed her heart when Geoffrey handed her down at the portico of Drury Lane Theatre. A new pantomime was a-foot. Geoffrey's father (that bluff red baron) had chartered a box, was already there with his lady and others.

Lily among peonies, Angelica sat brooding, her eyes fastened on the stage, Geoffrey behind her chair, brooding by the same token. Presto, he saw a flood of pink rush up her shoulders to her ears. The " principal boy" had just skipped on to the stage. No boy at all (God be witness), but one Mistress Tina Vandeleur, very apt in masquerado, and seeming true boy enough to the guileless. Stout of leg, light-footed, with a tricksy plume to his cap, and the swagger of one who would beard the Saints for a wager, this Aladdin was just such a galliard as Angelica had often fondled in her dreams. He lept straight into the closet of her heart, and " Deus ! " she cried, " maugre my maiden-hood, I will follow those pretty heels round the earth ! "

Cried Geoffrey " Yea ! and will not I presently string his ham to save your panting ? "

" *Tacete !* " cried the groundlings.

A moment after, Geoffrey forgot his spleen. Cupid had noosed him—bound him tight to the Widow Twankey. This was a woman most unlike to Angelica: poplar-tall, I grant you ; but elm-wide into the bargain ; deep-voiced, robustious, and puffed bravely out with hot vital essences. Seemed so to Geoffrey, at least, who had no smattering of theatres and knew not his cynosure to be none other than Master Willie Joffers, prime buffo of the day. Like Angelica, he had had fond visions ; and lo here, the very lady of them !

Says he to Angelica, " I am heartset on this widow."

" By so much the better ! " she laughs. " I to my peacock, you to your peahen, with a God-speed from each to other."

How to snare the birds ? A pretty problem : the fowling was like to be delicate. So hale a strutter as Aladdin could not lack for bonamies. " Will he deign me ? " wondered meek Angelica. " This widow," thought Geoffrey, " is belike no widow at all, but a modest wife with a yea for no man but her lord." Head to head they took counsel, cudgelled their wits for some proper vantage. Of a sudden, Geoffrey clapped hand to thigh. Student of Boccaccio, Heveletius, and other sages, he had the clue in his palm. A whisper from him, a nod from Angelica, and the twain withdrew from the box into the corridor without.

There, back to back, they disrobed swiftly, each tossing to other every garment as it was doffed. Then a flurried toilet, and a difficult, for the man especially ; but hotness of desire breeds dexterity. When they turned and faced each other, Angelica was such a boy as Aladdin would not spurn as page, Geoffrey such a girl as the widow might well covet as body-maid.

FOND HEARTS ASKEW

Out they hied under the stars, and sought way to the postern whereby the mummers would come when their work were done. Thereat they stationed themselves in shadow. A bitter night, with a lather of snow on the cobbles ; but they were heedless of that : love and their dancing hearts warmed them.

They waited long. Strings of muffled figures began to file out, but never an one like to Aladdin or the Widow. Midnight tolled. Had these two had wind of the ambuscado and crept out by another door ? Nay, patience !

At last ! A figure showed in the doorway—a figure cloaked womanly, but topped with face of Aladdin. Trousered Angelica, with a cry, darted forth from the shadow. To Mistress Vandeleur's eyes she was as truly man as was Mistress Vandeleur to hers. Thus confronted, Mistress Vandeleur shrank back, blushing hot.

" Nay ! " laughs Angelica, clipping her by the wrists. " Cold boy, you shall not so easily slip me. A pretty girl you make, Aladdin ; but love pierces such disguise as a rapier might pierce lard."

" Madman ! Unhandle me ! " screams the actress.

"No madman I, as well you know," answers Angelica, "but a maid whom spurned love may yet madden. Kiss me on the lips!"

While they struggle, another figure fills the postern, and in an instant Angelica is torn aside by Master Willie Joffers (well versed, for all his mumming, in matters of chivalry). "Kisses for such coward lips?" cries he. "Nay, but a swinge to silence them!" and would have struck trousered Angelica full on the mouth. But décolleté Geoffrey Dizzard, crying at him "Sweet termagant, think not to baffle me by these airs of manhood!" had sprung in the way and on his own nose received the blow.

He staggered and, spurting blood, fell. Up go the buffo's hands, and "Now may the Saints whip me," cries he, "for a tapster of girl's blood!" and fled into the night, howling like a dog. Mistress Vandeleur had fled already. Down on her knees goes Angelica, to stanch Geoffrey's flux.

Thus far, straight history. Apocrypha, all the rest: you shall pick your own sequel. As for instance, some say Geoffrey bled to the death, whereby stepped Master Joffers to the scaffold, and Angelica (the Vandeleur too, like as not) to a nunnery. Others have it he lived, thanks to nurse Angelica, who, thereon wed, suckled him twin Dizzards in due season. Joffers, they say, had wife already, else would have wed the Vandeleur, for sake of symmetry.

DICKENS

By

GR**GE M**RE

DICKENS

I HAD often wondered why when people talked
to me of Tintoretto I always found myself
thinking of Turgéneff. It seemed to me strange
that I should think of Turgéneff instead of
thinking of Tintoretto ; for at first sight nothing
can be more far apart than the Slav mind and
the Flemish. But one morning, some years ago,
while I was musing by my fireplace in Victoria
Street, Dolmetsch came to see me. He had a
soiled roll of music under his left arm. I said,
"How are you?" He said, "I am well. And
you?" I said, "I, too, am well. What is that,
my dear Dolmetsch, that you carry under your
left arm?" He answered, "It is a Mass by
Palestrina." "Will you read me the score?" I
asked. I was afraid he would say no. But
Dolmetsch is not one of those men who say no,
and he read me the score. He did not read very
well, but I had never heard it before, so when he
finished I begged of him he would read it to me
again. He said, "Very well, M✷✷re, I will read
it to you again." I remember his exact words,

179

because they seemed to me at the time to be the sort of thing that only Dolmetsch could have said. It was a foggy morning in Victoria Street, and while Dolmetsch read again the first few bars, I thought how Renoir would have loved to paint in such an atmosphere the tops of the plane trees that flaccidly show above the wall of Buckingham Palace. . . . Why had I never been invited to Buckingham Palace? I did not want to go there, but it would have been nice to have been asked. . . . How *brave gaillard* was Renoir, and how well he painted from that subfusc palette! . . .

My roving thoughts were caught back to the divine score which Arnold Dolmetsch was reading to me. How well placed they were, those semibreves! Could anyone but Palestrina have placed them so nicely? I wondered what girl Palestrina was courting when he conceived them. She must have been blonde, surely, and with narrow flanks. . . . There are moments when one does not think of girls, are there not, dear reader? And I swear to you that such a moment came to me while Dolmetsch mumbled the last two bars of that Mass. The notes were " do, la, sol, do, fa, do, sol, la," and as he mumbled them I sat upright and stared into space, for it had become suddenly plain to me why when people talked of Tintoretto I always found myself thinking of Turgéneff.

I do not say that this story that I have told to you is a very good story, and I am afraid that I have not well told it. Some day, when I have time, I should like to re-write it. But meantime I let it stand, because without it you could not receive what is upmost in my thoughts, and which I wish you to share with me. Without it, what I am yearning to say might seem to you a hard saying; but now you will understand me.

There never was a writer except Dickens. Perhaps you have never heard say of him? No matter, till a few days past he was only a name to me. I remember that when I was a young man in Paris, I read a praise of him in some journal; but in those days I was kneeling at other altars, I was scrubbing other doorsteps. . . . So has it been ever since; always a false god, always the wrong doorstep. I am sick of the smell of the incense I have swung to this and that false god—Zola, Yeats, *et tous ces autres*. I am angry to have got housemaid's knee, because I got it on doorsteps that led to nowhere. There is but one doorstep worth scrubbing. The doorstep of Charles Dickens. . . .

Did he write many books ? I know not, it does not greatly matter, he wrote the "Pickwick Papers"; that suffices. I have read as yet but one chapter, describing a Christmas party in a country house. Strange that anyone should have essayed to write about anything but that ! Christmas—I see it now—is the only moment in which men and women are really alive, are really worth writing about. At other seasons they do not exist for the purpose of art. I spit on all seasons except Christmas. . . Is he not in all fiction the greatest figure, this Mr. Wardell, this old "squire" rosy-cheeked, who entertains this Christmas party at his house ? He is more truthful, he is more significant, than any figure in Balzac. He is better than all Balzac's figures rolled into one. . . I used to kneel on that doorstep. Balzac wrote many books. But now it behoves me to ask myself whether he ever wrote a good book. One knows that he used to write for fifteen hours at a stretch, gulping down coffee all the while. But it does not follow that the coffee was good, nor does it follow that what he wrote was good. The

DICKENS

Comédie Humaine is all chicory. . . I had wished for some years to say this, I am glad *d'avoir débarrassé ma poitrine de ça.*

To have described divinely a Christmas party is something, but it is not everything. The disengaging of the erotic motive is everything, is the only touchstone. If while that is being done we are soothed into a trance, a nebulous delirium of the nerves, then we know the novelist to be a supreme novelist. If we retain consciousness, he is not supreme, and to be less than supreme in art is to not exist. . . Dickens disengages the erotic motive through two figures, Mr. Winkle, a sportman, and Miss Arabella, "a young lady with fur-topped boots." They go skating, he helps her over a stile. Can one not well see her? She steps over the stile and her shin defines itself through her balbriggan stocking. She is a knock-kneed girl, and she looks at Mr. Winkle with that sensual regard that sometimes comes when the wind is north-west. Yes, it is a northwest wind that is blowing over this landscape that Hals or Winchoven might have painted—no, Winchoven would have fumbled it with rose-madder, but Hals would have done it well. Hals would have approved—would he not?—the pollard

aspens, these pollard aspens deciduous and
wistful, which the rime makes glistening. That
field, how well ploughed it is, and are they not
like petticoats, those clouds low-hanging ? Yes,
Hals would have stated them well, but only
Manet could have stated the slope of the thighs
of the girl—how does she call herself ?—Arabella
—it is a so hard name to remember—as she steps
across the stile. Manet would have found
pleasure in her cheeks also. They are a little
chapped with the north-west wind that makes the
pollard aspens to quiver. How adorable a thing
it is, a girl's nose that the north-west wind renders
red ! We may tire of it sometimes, because we
sometimes tire of all things, but Winkle does not
know this. Is Arabella his mistress ? If she is
not, she has been, or at any rate she will be.
How full she is of temperament, is she not ? Her
shoulder-blades seem a little carelessly modelled,
but how good they are in intention ! How well
placed that smut on her left cheek !

Strange thoughts of her surge up vaguely in me
as I watch her—thoughts that I cannot express
in English. . . Elle est plus vieille que les roches
entre lesquelles elle s'est assise ; comme le vampire
elle a été fréquemment morte, et a appris les

secrets du tombeau ; et s'est plongée dans des mers profondes, et conserve autour d'elle leur jour ruiné ; et, comme Lède, était mère d'Hélène de Troie, et, comme Sainte-Anne, mère de Maria ; et tout cela n'a été pour elle que. . . . I desist, for not through French can be expressed the thoughts that surge in me. French is a stale language. So are all the European languages, one can say in them nothing fresh. . . . The stalest of them all is Erse. . . .

Deep down in my heart a sudden voice whispers me that there is only one land wherein art may reveal herself once more. Of what avail to await her anywhere else than in Mexico ? Only there can the apocalypse happen. I will take a ticket for Mexico, I will buy a Mexican grammar, I will be a Mexican. . . . On a hillside, or beside some grey pool, gazing out across those plains poor and arid, I will await the first pale showings of the new dawn. . . .

EUPHEMIA CLASHTHOUGHT

AN IMITATION OF MEREDITH

EUPHEMIA CLASHTHOUGHT [1]

IN the heart of insular Cosmos, remote by some scores of leagues of Hodge-trod arable or pastoral, not more than a snuff-pinch for gaping tourist nostrils accustomed to inhalation of prairie winds, but enough for perspective, from those marginal sands, trident-scraped, we are to fancy, by a helmeted Dame Abstract familiarly profiled on discs of current bronze—price of a loaf for humbler maws disdainful of Gallic side-dishes for the titillation of choicer palates—stands Clash-thought Park, a house of some pretension, mentioned at Runnymede, with the spreading exception of wings given to it in later times by Daedalean masters not to be baulked of billiards or traps for Terpsichore, and owned for

[1] It were not, as a general rule, well to republish after a man's death the skit you made of his work while he lived. Meredith, however, was so transcendent that such skits must ever be harmless, and so lasting will his fame be that they can never lose what freshness they may have had at first. So I have put this thing in with the others, making improvements that were needed.—M. B.

unbroken generations by a healthy line of procreant Clashthoughts, to the undoing of collateral
branches eager for the birth of a female. Pas-
sengers through cushioned space, flying top-
speed or dallying with obscure stations not
alighted at apparently, have had it pointed out
to them as beheld dimly for a privileged instant
before they sink back behind crackling barrier of
instructive paper with a "Thank you, Sir," or
"Madam," as the case may be. Guide-books
praise it. I conceive they shall be studied for a
cock-shy of rainbow epithets slashed in at the
target of Landed Gentry, premonitorily. The
tintinnabulation's enough. Periodical footings of
Clashthoughts into Mayfair or the Tyrol, sig-
nalled by the slide from its mast of a crested
index of Aeolian caprice, blazon of their presence,
give the curious a right to spin through the
halls and galleries under a cackle of housekeeper
guideship—scramble for a chuck of the dainties,
dog fashion. There is something to be said for
the rope's twist. Wisdom skips.

It is recorded that the goblins of this same
Lady Wisdom were all agog one Christmas
morning between the doors of the house and the
village church, which crouches on the outskirt of

the park, with something of a lodge in its look, you might say, more than of celestial twinkles, even with Christmas hoar-frost bleaching the grey of it in sunlight, as one sees imaged on seasonable missives for amity in the trays marked " sixpence and upwards," here and there, on the counters of barter.

Be sure these goblins made obeisance to Sir Peter Clashthought, as he passed by, starched beacon of squirearchy, wife on arm, sons to heel. After him, certain members of the household— rose-chapped males and females, bearing books of worship. The pack of goblins glance up the drive with nudging elbows and whisperings of " Where is daughter Euphemia ? Where Sir Rebus, her affianced ? "

Off they scamper for a peep through the windows of the house. They throng the sill of the library, ears acock and eyelids twittering admiration of a prospect. Euphemia was in view of them—essence of her. Sir Rebus was at her side. Nothing slips the goblins.

" Nymph in the Heavy Dragoons " was Mrs. Cryptic-Sparkler's famous definition of her. The County took it for final—an uncut gem with a fleck in the heart of it. Euphemia condoned the

A CHRISTMAS GARLAND

imagery. She had breadth. Heels that spread ample curves over the ground she stood on, and hands that might floor you with a clench of them, were hers. Grey eyes looked out lucid and fearless under swelling temples that were lost in a ruffling copse of hair. Her nose was virginal, with hints of the Iron Duke at most angles. Square chin, cleft centrally, gave her throat the look of a tower with a gun protrudent at top. She was dressed for church evidently, but seemed no slave to Time. Her bonnet was pushed well back from her head, and she was fingering the ribbons. One saw she was a woman. She inspired deference.

"Forefinger for Shepherd's Crook" was what Mrs. Cryptic-Sparkler had said of Sir Rebus. It shall stand at that.

"You have Prayer Book?" he queried.

She nodded. Juno catches the connubial trick.

"Hymns?"

"Ancient and Modern."

"I may share with you?"

"I know by heart. Parrots sing."

"Philomel carols," he bent to her.

"Complaints spoil a festival."

192

EUPHEMIA CLASHTHOUGHT

He waved hand to the door. "Lady, your father has started."

"He knows the adage. Copy-books instil it."

"Inexorable truth in it."

"We may dodge the scythe."

"To be choked with the sands?"

She flashed a smile. "I would not," he said, "that my Euphemia were late for the Absolution."

She cast eyes to the carpet. He caught them at the rebound.

"It snows," she murmured, swimming to the window.

"A flake, no more. The season claims it."

"I have thin boots."

"Another pair?"

"My maid buttons. She is at church."

"My fingers?"

"Ten on each."

"Five," he corrected.

"Buttons."

"I beg your pardon."

She saw opportunity. She swam to the bell-rope and grasped it for a tinkle. The action spread feminine curves to her lover's eyes. He was a man.

Obsequiousness loomed in the doorway. Its

mistress flashed an order for port—two glasses.
Sir Rebus sprang a pair of eyebrows on her.
Suspicion slid down the banisters of his mind,
trailing a blue ribbon. Inebriates were one of
his hobbies. For an instant she was sunset.

" Medicinal," she murmured.

" Forgive me, Madam. A glass, certainly.
'Twill warm us for worshipping."

The wine appeared, seemed to blink owlishly
through the facets of its decanter, like some hoary
captive dragged forth into light after years of
subterraneous darkness—something querulous in
the sudden liberation of it. Or say that it
gleamed benignant from its tray, steady-borne by
the hands of reverence, as one has seen Infallibility
pass with uplifting of jewelled fingers through
genuflexions to the Balcony. Port has this in it :
that it compels obeisance, master of us ; as opposed
to brother and sister wines wooing us with a coy
flush in the gold of them to a cursory tope or
harlequin leap shimmering up the veins with a
sly wink at us through eyelets. Hussy vintages
swim to a cosset. We go to Port, mark you !

Sir Rebus sipped with an affectionate twirl of
thumb at the glass's stem. He said " One scents
the cobwebs."

" Catches in them," Euphemia flung at him.

" I take you.   Bacchus laughs in the web."

" Unspun but for Pallas."

" A lady's jealousy."

" Forethought, rather."

" Brewed in the paternal pate.   Grant it ! "

" For a spring in accoutrements."

Sir Rebus inclined gravely.   Port precludes prolongment of the riposte.

She replenished glasses.   Deprecation yielded. " A step," she said, " and we are in time for the First Lesson."

" This," he agreed, " is a wine."

" There are blasphemies in posture.   One should sit to it."

" Perhaps."   He sank to commodious throne of leather indicated by her finger.

Again she filled for him.   " This time, no heel-taps," she was imperative.   " The Litany demands basis."

" True."   He drained, not repelling the decanter placed at his elbow.

" It is a wine," he presently repeated with a rolling tongue over it.

" Laid   down   by   my   great-grandfather. Cloistral."

"Strange," he said, examining the stopper, "no date. Antediluvian. Sound, though."

He drew out his note-book. "*The senses,*" he wrote, "*are internecine. They shall have learned esprit de corps before they enslave us.*" This was one of his happiest flings to general from particular. "*Visual distraction cries havoc to ultimate delicacy of palate*" would but have pinned us a butterfly best a-hover; nor even so should we have had truth of why the aphorist, closing note-book and nestling back of head against that of chair, closed eyes also.

As by some such law as lurks in meteorological toy for our guidance in climes close-knit with Irony for bewilderment, making egress of old woman synchronise inevitably with old man's ingress, or the other way about, the force that closed the aphorist's eye-lids parted his lips in degree according. Thus had Euphemia, erect on hearth-rug, a cavern to gaze down into. Outworks of fortifying ivory cast but denser shadows into the inexplorable. The solitudes here grew murmurous. To and fro through secret passages in the recesses leading up deviously to lesser twin caverns of nose above, the gnomes Morphean went about their business, whispering at first, but

196

presently bold to wind horns in unison—Roland-wise, not less.

Euphemia had an ear for it; whim also to construe lord and master relaxed but reboant and soaring above the verbal to harmonic truths of abstract or transcendental, to be hummed subsequently by privileged female audience of one bent on a hook-or-crook plucking out of pith for salvation.

She caught tablets pendent at her girdle. "*How long*," queried her stilus, "*has our sex had humour? Jael hammered.*"

She might have hitched speculation further. But Mother Earth, white-mantled, called to her.

Casting eye of caution at recumbence, she paddled across the carpet and anon swam out over the snow.

Pagan young womanhood, six foot of it, spanned eight miles before luncheon.

960506B   27.50 (8.25)